D1827721

AMSTERDAM STUDIES IN CLASSICAL PHILOLOGY

EDITORS

ALBERT RIJKSBARON

IRENE J.F. DE JONG   HARM PINKSTER

VOLUME EIGHT

PREVIOUSLY PUBLISHED

LATIN IN USE
AMSTERDAM STUDIES
IN THE PRAGMATICS OF LATIN

EDITED BY

RODIE RISSELADA

J.C. GIEBEN, PUBLISHER

AMSTERDAM 1998

ISBN 90 5063 297 1 / Printed in The Netherlands

Preface

The five *Studies in the Pragmatics of Latin* that are collected in this volume are all based on papers that were read at the *International Colloquia on Latin Linguistics* which were held in Eichstätt in 1995 (Bolkestein, De Jong, Pinkster, Risselada) and in Madrid in 1997 (Kroon). There were, at that time, various good, practical reasons for publishing our papers in a separate volume, such as time (a motive which, unfortunately, has lost its relevance over the years) and the length of the papers.

The main idea behind this volume is, however, not of a practical nature, but concerns the common approach that characterizes the papers that are brought together here. As is reflected in the title, they all contribute to the study of Latin pragmatics. Even if the papers by De Jong (on *iste*) and Pinkster (on the present tense) deal with questions that are partly semantic, they focus on the actual use of these phenomena in Latin texts and, like the other three papers, they are based on extensive corpus research. There are, furthermore, various connections between the subject matter of individual papers. Both Kroon and Pinkster deal with tense and narrative structure, while the papers by Kroon and Risselada share an interest in discourse particles. The paper by Bolkestein explores a somewhat different and hitherto neglected area of Latin pragmatics, viz. parenthetical clauses.

Last but not least, we hope that this small collection of Amsterdam papers on pragmatics gives an indication of our fruitful collaboration in Latin linguistics over the last years.

We are grateful to Albert Rijksbaron, series editor of the *Amsterdam Studies in Classical Philology*, who meticulously read the final proofs and corrected a number of minor and major errors.

Contents

Between brackets: (some properties of) parenthetical clauses in Latin. An investigation of the language of Cicero's letters

A. Machtelt Bolkestein

In this paper I examine the distribution of two categories of parenthetical expressions in Cicero's letters: parenthetical full clauses and parenthetically used modalizing mental state verbs. It is shown that these two categories differ with respect to the degree to which they are sensitive to distribution of information in the host clause. The first category always occurs preceding the main Focus of the host clause, thus in a sense postponing the pragmatic completion of the clause; for the second category the location of the main Focus in the host clause is not relevant. On the basis of several parameters it is furthermore shown that the latter category is less homogeneous than is commonly taken for granted, and that the parenthetical use of these mental state verbs is not always parallel to their use as main verbs.

0. Introduction

There is little research about parenthetical expressions, both in the general linguistic litterature (recent exceptions are Ziv 1985; Espinal 1991; Brandt 1994 and Pittner 1995) and in Latin linguistics (exceptions: Roschatt 1883; Von Albrecht 1964; and, on parenthetical verba dicendi only, Risselada 1989). Apart from the fact that linguistics in the past has focussed on 'idealized' well formed sentences rather than on the presumed 'imperfections' of sentences in spoken language, one of the reasons for this lack of attention may be that there are very few restrictions on the type of linguistic expression which can be parenthetically inserted into some host clause. That is, we may find adjectival and adverbial phrases, appositional noun phrases, exclamations, curses, expanding relative clauses, various kinds of subordinate clauses, modalizing verbs of cognition, speech act modifying verbs of speech, and syntactically full clauses which do not differ from ordinary main clauses, etc.

 Criteria for when to classify an expression as being parenthetical are flexible too: they may be prosodic and/or syntactic and/or semantic and/or pragmatic (or: discourse-functional). There is some consensus concerning prosodic criteria: parentheticals are not integrated into the intonational contour of the host clause; if they are full clauses, they have their own intonational contour, they may be accompanied by pauses, and they are often pronounced at a speed or pitch which is different from their host clause. Syntactically, they are said to be independent, that is, their presence is claimed not to have any consequences for the syntactic properties of the host clause (unless the latter becomes an anacoluthon as a result of being disturbed by the parenthesis), and, the other way round, they are claimed not themselves to be sensitive to any syntactic rules which apply to the host unit. They also are (relatively) free as to the position they may occupy in their host.[1] Semantically they may have any of a large number of semantic (or: 'logical') relations — whether or not explicitated by the presence of subordinating conjunctions, particles or other discourse markers — with respect to their host, and the same holds for their 'pragmatic' (or: rhetorical, see Matthiessen & Thompson 1988) functions in the discourse: this, of course, leads to the eternal decision problem of how far to go in distinguishing such relations.

In the present paper I will examine and compare two distinct subcategories of parenthetical expressions in Latin discourse, taking as a sample Cicero's letters (because of their relatively colloquial style). The first type I will examine consists of parenthetical 'full' clauses which are enclosed within their host clause, as exemplified in (1). This formulation implies that I leave out of account those clauses which either precede or follow another full clause, and those which have the syntactic characteristics of a subordinate satellite clause or of a relative clause, as in (2). Though the description of the category under examination sounds simple enough, some dubious cases remain. I have included instances like the ones in (3) because of reasons to be specified below (section 2).

(1)   a. sed, cum ..., exarsi non solum praesenti, credo, iracundia (nam ea tam
           vehemens fortasse non fuisset), sed cum inclusum illud odium ..., omne
           repente apparuit. (Cic. *Fam.* 1.9.20)
           'but, when ..., I was inflamed not only with my current, I believe, anger
           (for that would perhaps not have been so vehement), but, since that pent-
           up hate ..., all of it suddenly appeared.'
      b. primum hoc velim existimes ...; deinde, si ..., ut mihi ignoscas (tam enim
           sum amicus rei publicae quam qui maxime); si vero ..., satis habeas ... (Cic.
           Fam. 5.2.6)
           'first I would like you to think this ...; then, if ..., for you to forgive me
           (for I am just as great a friend of the state as the greatest); but if ..., for
           you to be satisfied ...'
      c. cuius ego iudicium, pace tua dixerim, longe antepono tuo. (Cic. *Tusc.* 5.12)
           'whose judgment, if I may say so with your permission, I value much
           more than yours.'

---

1. On closer observation, these generalizations need to be modified for certain subtypes of parentheticals, see Espinal (1991), Pittner (1995) and Ziv (1985).

(2) a. Etsi statueram nullas ad te litteras mittere nisi commendaticias (non quo eas intellegerem satis apud te valere, sed ne ... ostenderem), tamen ... putavi ... (Cic. *Fam.* 5.5.1)

'Although I had decided not to send you any other letters than recommendations (not because I understood that those were rather effective with you, but in order not to show ...), still I thought ...'

b. Rem enim — quod te non fugit — magnam complexus sum et plurimi otii, quo ego maxime egeo. (Cic. *Att.* 4.16.2)

'An enormous undertaking — which does not escape you — and of a lot of free time, which I especially lack, I have taken upon me.'

(3) a. Res ante Idus acta sic est (nam haec Idibus mane scripsi): Hortensi ... sententia cedit religioni de exercitu; (Cic. *Fam.* 1.1.3)

'The situation before the fifteenth has gone as follows (for I wrote this letter on the fifteenth early in the morning): Hortensius' ... proposal concerning the army makes way for the fear;'

b. Nam si ..., Ciliciam quidem ipsam ... facile tenuissem (duo enim sunt aditus in Ciliciam ...), sed me Cappadocia movebat, ... (Cic. *Fam.* 15.4.4)

'For if ..., I easily could have held Cilicia itself (there are, as you know, two ways to enter into Cilicia ...), but I was motivated by Cappadocia, ...'

c. Perspice aequitatem animi mei et ... et mehercule cum Caesare suavissimam coniunctionem (haec enim me una ex hoc naufragio tabula delectat). Qui quidem Quintum meum ... quemadmodum tractat honore ...! (Cic. *Att.* 4.19.2)

'See the calmness of my mind and ... by god my most agreeable relation with Caesar (for that is the only piece of wood from the whole shipwreck which delights me). And how does he treat my Quintus ... with honour ...!'

The second subcategory of parenthetical expressions which I will discuss are what I call 'modalizing' *verba sentiendi* (mental state verbs), the latter both when introduced by the subordinator *ut* 'as' and when lacking such a subordinator. Syntactically, when not introduced by *ut*, such expressions are not full clauses, because their second argument slot (that of the complement clause) is not filled (although semantically, the host clause contains the modalized proposition). They are exemplified by *credo* in (1a) above and in (4a), and by *ut ego arbitror*, *opinor* and *ut ego existimo* in (4a-c):

(4) a. Sed quoniam primus annus ..., credo propterea quod tibi ... intolerabilis
         videbatur, secundus autem multo lenior ..., quod et ... et, ut ego arbitror,
         meae quoque litterae te patientiorem ... fecerunt (Cic. *Q. fr.* 1.1.40)
         'But since the first year ..., I believe because ... seemed to you intolerable,
         (and since) the second year was much more agreeable, because both ...
         and, at least that is my opinion, my own letters too have made you more
         tolerant'
     b. Melitam igitur, opinor, capessamus, dum quid in Hispania. (Cic. *Att.*
         10.9.1)
         'So let us then take Melita, I think, as long as (we take) something in
         Spain.'
     c. Quod si iste Italiam relinquet, faciet omnino male et, ut ego existimo,
         alogistoos, sed tum demum consilia nostra commutanda erunt. (Cic. *Att.*
         9.10.4)
         'But if that man will leave Italy, he will act wrongly and, to my mind,
         irrationally, but then and not till then will be the time to change our
         plans.'

The main question I will investigate is whether or not there are restrictions as to
the position which these two categories of parenthetical expressions may occupy
in Latin. The answer will turn out to differ for the two categories: it will be in the
affirmative at least for the first type, but for this category it will have to be
formulated in terms of discourse-functional notions rather than in syntactic terms,
whereas for the second type a semantic qualification seems to be adequate.[2]

1. Parenthesis in Ovidius

Von Albrecht (1964) has investigated (all?) 179 instances of parenthetical
expressions in Ovidius' *Metamorphoses*, giving an extensive survey of some of their
internal syntactic and metrical properties, their syntactic and metrical position and
their 'logical' or 'rhetorical' function with respect to their host clause. The attested
instances discussed include parentheses consisting of single words and word phrases,
some kinds of subordinate clauses, whole independent clauses and so on. From Von

---

2. I am not going into the various semantic and rhetorical functions which full clause parentheses
may fulfill with respect to their host clause. In both Ovidius' *Met.* and in Cicero's letters a majority
is introduced by some causal connector, such as *nam* or *enim*, with the functions described for
these discourse connectives in Kroon (1985). *Enim* seems to be relatively more frequent within
parenthesis than *nam* in both samples, something which fits in nicely with its more interactive
nature.

Albrecht's data it can be observed that in Ovidius roughly 50% of the cases of full clause parenthesis occur at a 'syntactic break', that is, at a borderline between two clauses: this may be between two coordinated clauses of the same level, as e.g. main and main clause (including cases of two coordinated predicates with the same Subject), or subordinate and subordinate clause, or it may be at the borderline between a main and a subordinate clause or — more often — between a subordinate and a main clause. The other half of the cases in Ovidius do not occur at a syntactic break but within a nuclear clause: some occur right after the first constituent of the host clause, and the rest somewhere in the middle of the host clause, between a Subject and the verb or between an Object and the verb or between some (nominal or prepositional) satellite and the verb and so on.[3] Since Latin word order is flexible, verbs may precede all of these nuclear and satellite constituents as well. Clause internal parenthesis of course also includes a number (12x) of cases where the parenthesis occurs between a nominal constituent and its attributive modifier (which may precede [10x] or follow [2x] the noun); or between an adjective or participle which is used predicatively and either the nominal constituent with which it agrees or the verb (in case of non-expression of the Head).[4] The two types of 'Sperrung' (hyperbaton) are illustrated in (5a-b):[5]

(5)   a. ... Gelidus nutricis in artus
         ossaque (sensit enim) penetrat tremor (Ov. *Met.* 10.423)
         'Cold horror stole through the limbs of the nurse and her bones (for she understood)'
    b. Talia nequiquam questus (nam cuncta videbam)
        surgit ... (Ov. *Met.* 13.870)

---

3. I regard parentheses occurring between a complement and its predicate as not being at a syntactic break, even if these complements are finite clauses (of course in Latin many complements are not finite, such as the Accusative plus Infinitive clauses). On the other hand, I have registered satellites which are noun phrases or prepositional phrases also as not forming a break, whereas if such satellites are realized as finite clauses I view them as forming a syntactic break, in spite of the fact that they semantically fulfill the same function as non-finite forms. This view is disputable, but defendable on the grounds that (statistically) NPs and PPs are more frequently 'embraced' on all sides by the nuclear clause than are satellites realized as finite clauses. As is claimed in Dik (1989), there is a language universal tendency for syntactically 'heavy' constituents to occur later in the clause. This holds for Latin as well.
4. Von Albrecht (1964) does not systematically distinguish between the attributive and predicative use of adjectives or participles.
5. In Ovidius, metrical considerations may have had some impact on where the parenthesis is inserted (such a claim, however, is never falsifiable). Also, since Complement clauses in Latin may be either non-finite infinitival clauses or finite clauses introduced by some subordinator such as *ut* or *quod* (see note 3), the number of parentheses found at a 'syntactic break' might vary from the the number given in Von Albrecht (1964) according to the criteria used; the general conclusion, however, will be much the same (in view of the findings in Cicero's letters to be discussed below).

'Uttering such vain complaints (for I saw it all) he rose ...'

Furthermore, there are no occurrences in Ovidius of a parenthesis between a preposition and the noun (phrase) governed by it, as in (6):

(6)   ?? his dictis ad — nam nox erat — castra profectus est
       'after these words he left for — since it was night — the camp'

The restriction illustrated in (6) seems to hold for languages in general. For languages which possess definite and indefinite articles, it is sometimes claimed that parentheses are excluded from the position between determiner and noun as well (Espinal 1991: 752). However, as Pittner (1995) shows for German on the basis of attested instances in journalistic discourse, this claim does not hold for parentheses of a specific type, namely those which are a metalinguistic comment, that is, which justify the speaker's choice of words. I have found only one attested case of full clause parenthesis in between a determiner and its Head noun in Ovidius (7a), but none in Cicero's letters. However, a case like (7b) does not seem impossible to me, whereas a case like (7c) seems less acceptable:[6]

(7)   a. Hoc me, nate dea, (quis possit credere?) telum
          flere facit ... (Ov. *Met.* 7.690)
          'This weapon, son of a goddess, (who could believe it?) makes me
          weep ...'
       b. ?ille — pace tua dixerim — amicus tuus mihi non persuadet
          'that — forgive me for saying this — friend of yours does not convince
          me'
       c. ??ille — nam nox erat — amicus tuus ad castra profectus est
          'that — for it was night — friend of yours left for the camp'

---

6. Among the instances of parenthesis within an NP in Ovidius four concern possessive adjectives. One dubious case from Cicero's letters with a parenthesis, which, however, is itself not a full clause, inserted between Head and determiner is:
   Cn. Octavius est — an Cn. Cornelius — quidam (or: — an Cn. Cornelius quidam —),
   tuus familiaris ... Is me ... invitat (Cic. *Fam.* 7.9.3)
to be interpreted as either 'there is a certain Cn. Octavius — or Cn. Cornelius — , an acquaintance of yours ... He invites me' or: 'there is a Cn. Octavius — or a certain Cn. Cornelius —' etc. Here it is not clear whether the determiner *quidam* belongs to the first proper name or to the second, or to both (the following apposition applies to either of the two). Moreover, short phrases such as the one here introduced by *an* are not as recognizably parenthetical as are full clauses, and perhaps do not necessarily manifest the prosodic phenomena associated with parenthetical clauses.

In view of the relative freedom allowed for word order in Latin poetic texts, we might expect to find word order phenomena in Ovidius' poems which deviate from the patterns occurring in ordinary discourse. However, it should be realized that discontinuity of a nominal constituent and its modifier as illustrated in (5a) may in fact occur in narrative prose as well, and if so, is in that case employed for specific pragmatic reasons (for conditions see De Jong 1986). I have mentioned the data from Ovidius in order to provide some background to which the language of Cicero's letters can be compared.

2. Parenthetical full clauses in Cicero's letters

In the prose of the letters, instances of parenthetical full clauses occurring at a syntactic break, such as (8a-b), outnumber (79 = 58%) those in which there is no break, such as (1c) above and (9a-b) (54 = 40%), but both are frequent.

(8) a. Quod si a te non impetro, hoc est, si quae te res impedierit (neque enim fas esse ...), cogar fortasse facere quod ... (Cic. *Fam.* 5.12.8)
'But if I fail to induce you to grant me this request, by which I mean, if anything prevents your doing so (for it is inconceivable to me that ...), I shall perhaps be forced to do what ...'
b. Cum ..., mihi facta statim est gratulatio (nemo enim dubitabat ...), cum subito ille in contionem escendit ... (Cic. *Att.* 4.2.3)
'When ..., I was immediately congratulated (for no one doubted ...), when suddenly he climbed the stage to hold a public meeting ...'

(9) a. Tuus autem ille amicus (scin quem ...? de quo ...) nos ... diligit ... (Cic. *Att.* 1.13.4)
'That friend of yours however (you know whom ...? about whom ...) ... loves us ...'
b. quod inimicum meum (meum autem? immo vero legum ...) sic amplexabantur, sic ... ut ... (Cic. *Fam.* 1.9.10)
'because they embrace my enemy (mine? no, of the law ...!) in such a way, in such a way ... that ...'
c. Sed (balbi non sumus) ad rem redeamus. (Cic. *Fam.* 2.10.1)
'But (we are not stammerers) let us come back to the business.'

I do not further subdivide in detail between which nuclear and satellite elements the clause-internal parentheses occur: about 20% of them occur immediately after the first position of the clause, and by far the majority occurs between an argument of the main predicate and the predicate itself (as in 9a-b). The biggest difference with the data from poetry is the fact that there are only very few instances (3 = 2%) of full clause parenthesis occurring between a noun and its modifier.[7] I quote the only instances attested in (10):

(10)   a. cum interea, credo equidem, malevoli homines (late enim patet hoc vitium et est in multis), sed tamen probabilem materiam nacti sermonis, ignari ... conabantur ... (Cic. *Fam.* 3.6.4)
'while in the meantime, I for my part believe, spiteful people (for everywhere that vice is apparent and it is present in many), but still having gotten plausible things to talk about, unaware ... tried to ...'

   b. id cum ipsius causa (est mihi, ut scis, in amoribus) tum mehercule etiam rei publicae (Cic. *Fam.* 7.32.3)
'this not only in his own interest (he is, as you know, dear to me), but by god also in that of the state'

   c. Raras tuas quidem (fortasse enim non perferuntur) sed suavis accipio litteras (Cic. *Fam.* 2.13.1)
'Very few (for perhaps they are not conveyed) but pleasant letters I receive'

Syntactically (10a-b) can be represented as: Modifier 1 Head // Modifier 2, and (10c) as: Modifier 1 // Modifier 2 Head, with '//' representing the parenthetical clause. In other words, in all three cases of full clause parenthesis breaking up a noun phrase, we are actually dealing with a noun accompanied not by one but by two modifiers, which are separated by the parenthetical clause and contrastive to each other (with the Head preceding in 10a-b and following in 10c).

What is essential in (10), is the pragmatic function constellation in these clauses. The two modifiers involved in each case are not just coordinated, but are strongly contrasted with each other: they carry contrastive Focus, in the terminology of Functional Grammar (Dik 1989). This contrastive focality is clear from the presence of *sed tamen* (10a), *cum ... tum* (10b) and *quidem ... sed* in (10c) as well. In such cases, the second Focus is stronger than the first. This means that

---

7. An instance of hyperbaton in which the parenthesis is not a main clause but a subordinate clause, is:
    Primum te, hominem non solum sapientem, verum etiam (ut nunc loquimur) urbanum, non arbitrabar ... delectari (Cic. *Fam.* 3.8.3)
    'Firstly, I never supposed that you, a man not only of common sense, but also (to use the modern phrase) of culture, ... derived pleasure'
Such instances seem to obey the same principles as the full clause parenthesis, but I have not investigated them thoroughly. Note that here we are dealing with a metalinguistic comment comparable to (7b).

the circumstances which allow the breaking up of the NPs by a parenthetical clause are quite specific, and pragmatic in nature. This condition holds for the instances from the prose sample, and is not observable in Ovidius (see 5).

Now, consider instances where the parenthetical clause occurs at a syntactic break, as in (8a-b), and (11) below:

(11) a. Pompeius, quotienscumque me vidit (videt autem saepe), gratias tibi agit singulares. (Cic. *Fam*. 13.41.1)
        'Pompeius, whenever he sees me (and he sees me often), is extremely grateful to you.'
      b. Quibus si me relaxaro (nam ut plane exsolvam non postulo), te ipsum ... docebo profecto quid sit ... (Cic. *Fam*. 7.1.5)
        'And if I will have loosened myself (for I do not require that I really free myself), (then) I will surely inform you yourself, what is ...'

In complex sentences, as a rule each of the component clauses has its own clausal Focus. Thus, in (8a) there is Focus on a part of the first clause, a conditional clause (*non impetro*), reinforced by the reformulation in the second conditional clause (*impedierit*), but there also is Focus in the main clause (*cogar facere*). In the complex sentence as a whole the second Focus is the strongest one: it contributes the most salient information. Example (8b) differs from (8a) in that the main clause precedes the subordinate clause (in this case a so-called *cum*-inversum clause). However, in this case too both clauses have their own Focus (*gratulatio* and *in contionem escendit* respectively), and the strongest Focus in the complex sentence as a whole is situated after the parenthesis. For (11a-b) a similar analysis is possible. In fact, if all instances of parenthetical clauses at a syntactic break are analyzed as to their pragmatic function constellation, it turns out that there are no instances where the strongest Focus of the sentence does not follow but precedes the parenthesis.

When we turn to intra-clausal parenthesis, it turns out that there as well we are often dealing with a focal constituent both before and after the interruption; and in each case the stronger Focus follows the parenthesis. If the parenthesis occurs after the first position of the clause, as in (9c), this is always the case. In other words, I have not encountered instances where the first position is itself filled by the strongest Focus constituent (although this would in principle be possible in Latin, see Pinkster 1990). If there is more than one constituent preceding the parenthesis, one of these may be focal, as is the case in (10a-b), but even then the strongest Focus still has to follow.

Often, both in sentences containing inter-clausal parenthesis and in those where the parenthesis does not separate two clauses, the expectation of a Focus-still-to-come is already raised by the presence of a particle such as *quidem* in the first part of the host sentence (often followed by *sed* or *tantum*), or by the first member of sequences such as *et ... // et, nec ... // nec, non (solum) ... // sed (etiam), tum ... // cum, ut ... // ita, primum ... // deinde* etc. The parenthetical clause will then occur in front of the second member of the correlative pattern (indicated here by //). This can be seen in a number of the examples quoted above. Further examples are given in (12):

(12)   a.   primum Ap. Claudium senatui populoque Romano non Midaeensium
             testimonio (in ea enim civitate mentio facta est), sed sua sponte esse
             laudatum (Cic. *Fam.* 3.8.3)
             'firstly, that Appius Claudius had won credit in the eyes of the senate and
             the Roman people not on the strength of the testimony of the inhabitants
             of Midaeum (for that was the state in which the matter was mentioned),
             but by acting according to his nature'
       b.   inde ... in Italiam ... pervenimus eodemque vento postridie (id erat a.d. VII
             Kal. Dec.) ... Brundisium venimus (Cic. *Fam.* 16.9.2)
             'From there ... we arrived in Italy and the day after (that was the fifth of
             december) with the same wind we arrived at Brindisi'

In fact, the examples quoted in (3) above, which are disputable as cases of parenthesis because the clause preceding it looks like a syntactically complete clause, contain such 'expectation raisers' too: *sic* in (3a), *quidem* in (3b). In (3c) the expectation is not coded explicitly, but created by the exhortation to pay attention to a series of climactically ordered facts: the last one, *cum Caesare ... coniunctionem*, preceded by the interjection *mehercule*, is so surprising as to require some explanation (which follows after the parenthesis). It seems plausible to assume that the intonation contour of such a stretch of clauses would also contain an indication that something more is to come (colon intonation).[8] So pragmatically, the clauses before the parenthesis are not 'complete'. In spoken language the speaker would, so to speak, be 'holding the floor' just a little bit longer by inserting a parenthetical remark at such a point, and his interlocutor would violate politeness rules in taking over before the main Focus has been presented.

---

8. This instance would by some scholars probably be regarded as sentence internal parenthesis, because of the continuation with the relative pronoun *qui*, which might also be analyzed as introducing an expanding relative clause. However, both the fact that the antecedent is not in the immediately preceding clause and the exclamative illocutionary force of this 'relative' clause make it resemble an independent main clause. Cases where the relative pronoun skips a whole (background) clause to find its antecedent are relatively rare (apart from instances where the clauses in between are in indirect speech, and the referent is its producer, see Bolkestein 1996).

Thus, the position of parenthetical full clauses is sensitive to, and in fact severely limited by, the pragmatic function constellation of the host clause: it is acceptable as long as the most important focal information has not yet been presented.[9]

I will now investigate instances of parenthetical modalizing verba sentiendi in order to see whether this generalization holds for such parentheses as well.

3. Modalizing mental state verbs

In Cicero's letters a range of verba sentiendi, signifying 'I believe', 'I think', 'I am of the opinion' etc., is employed parenthetically, preceded by or without introductory *ut* 'as', as a modalization in one way or another of the degree of strength with which the speaker posits his utterance (usually a Declarative sentence with an assertive illocutionary force). The most frequent ones are *(ut) opinor* (4b), *credo* (1a, 4a), *arbitror, puto* and *existimo* (in that order of frequency), but *(ut) sentio* and *censeo* occur as well. Some further examples are given in (13):

(13) a. Quinti fratris epistulam ad te misi, non satis humane illam quidem respondentem meis litteris sed tamen quod tibi satis sit, ut equidem existimo. (Cic. *Att.* 13.47a.2)
          'I am sending my brother Q.'s letter to you, not a very kind answer to mine, but still what should satisfy you, as I believe.'
      b. Sed, opinor, excipiamus et expectemus (Cic. *Att.* 2.5.1)
          'But, I suppose, let us lie low and wait'
      c. Cuius modi velim, puto, quaeris. (Cic. *Fam.* 8.3.3)
          'What kind of thing I want, I suppose, you will ask.'
      d. neque, ut ego arbitror, errarent ne adversarii quidem eius ... (Cic. *Fam.* 1.8.2)
          'and, as I think, even his opponents would make no mistake ...'
      e. ut plus prosis amicis meis quam ego praesens fortasse prodessem, credo quod magis ego dubitarem ... (Cic. *Fam.* 13.27.2)
          'as to be of more service to my friends than perhaps I should be myself, were I on the spot, I believe because I would hesitate more ...'

9. An investigation of parenthetically used sentence appositions introduced by *id quod* 'something which' (litt. 'that which') in Cicero's letters shows that this subcategory manifests the same sensitivity to the distribution of topical and focal information in the host sentence (based on data collected by W. van Maanen). Cases of full clause parenthesis in Sen. *Ep.* also seem to obey this tendency (data collected by G. Ryntjes).

f. Non modo ibi non fuisti, ubi ..., sed eo discessisti, quo ego te ne persequi
quidem possem triginta diebus, qui tibi ad decedendum lege, ut opinor,
Cornelia constituti essent (Cic. *Fam.* 3.6.3)
'Not only were you not at the place where ..., but you went off to where
I could not even catch up with you within the thirty days which were
fixed, as I believe, by the Cornelian law as the limit of your stay'

Expressions like the above are common in other languages as well (in a language
like Dutch or German such a parenthetical use of mental state verbs without a
subordinating conjunction will have VS order, as opposed to the SV order of
Declarative main clauses). They tend to be treated as a homogeneous group, and
are often put on a par with modalizing sentential adverbs of the type 'perhaps',
'surely', etc.[10]

If we compare the distribution of parenthetical modalizing verba sentiendi
to that of parenthetical full clauses with respect to linear position and with respect
to their sensitivity to pragmatic function constellation, they show quite a
difference. Firstly, they occur relatively less frequently (roughly 7% of the instances
in the sample) at a syntactic break between two clauses (one example is 13e).
Secondly, they are relatively much more frequent immediately after the first
position of the clause, as e.g. in (13b) and (13d): this is the case in roughly 42% of
the instances. Thirdly, among the 102 instances which I collected, quite a number
(especially of *credo* and *[ut] opinor*) occur between a modifier and its Head, as e.g.
in (13f) and (1a) above (10% of the instances). As a rule, in such cases the scope of
the modalization is limited to only one constituent of the NP, e.g. the Modifier
alone, as in (13f) and (1a), or the Head alone. In the other cases (as when they
occur in or immediately after the first position) their scope may be the whole
clause (as in 13b and 13d), or it may be part of the clause, and in the latter case it
may be the following part (as in 13e) or the preceding one (as in 13a).

With respect to the distribution of pragmatic functions in the sentence as a
whole, obviously in instances where the modalizing verb occurs in first position
or immediately after elements which obligatorily fill the first position such as
conjunctions, the main Focus still has to follow. In all other instances it is
theoretically possible that the main Focus of the sentence as a whole precedes the
modalizing expression. This is indeed the case in many instances, for example in
(13e) above, and of course in all cases where the modalizing verb is attached to the
end of the sentence as in (13a). When the verb is inserted within an NP between

---

10. Some of them may be strongly grammaticalized: thus in some varieties of Dutch (such as the
West-Frisian dialect spoken in North-Holland) the expression *denk ik*, litt. 'think I', may be realized
without an explicit Subject as *denk*.

a Modifier and its Head, the main Focus of the clause may precede it as well, as in (13f), where the main Focus falls on the second member of the contrast between *ibi ... ubi* 'here ... where' and *eo ... quo* 'to that place ... where'. In other words, the location of such modalizing verbs is not sensitive to the general pragmatic function constellation of the host utterance as a whole (although, of course, the modalization provides the modalized entity falling under its scope with some degree of focality): as we have argued above, full clause parenthesis always precedes the main Focus of the sentence.

Not only does this subclass of parentheticals exhibit properties different from that of parenthetical full clauses, but there are further differences in behaviour within the group of verba sentiendi as well. Four parameters in which they mutually differ are (i) the presence or absence of introductory *ut*; (ii) the presence or absence of emphasizing *ego* or *equidem*;[11] (iii) the type of syntactic/semantic unit involved; and (iv) the possibility to occur in a non-Declarative host clause.

Ad (i): it turns out that *credo* is never preceded by the subordinator, whereas *arbitror* and (less frequently occurring) *sentio* always are. The verbs *(ut) puto, opinor, existimo* occur both with and — somewhat less frequently — without the subordinating conjunction.

Ad (ii): it turns out that *puto* and *opinor* never, and *credo* almost never occur with emphasizing *ego/equidem* (the only example I encountered where *credo* is accompanied by it is 10a above), whereas *ut sentio* always, and *ut arbitror* very often (as in 13d) are accompanied by it. *Existimo* occurs both with (see 13a and 4c above) and without it.

A global examination of authors other than Cicero (Plautus, Terentius, Petronius, Seneca *Epistulae* and Apuleius) shows that these differences in behaviour manifest themselves elsewhere as well. This suggests that the class of expressions involved is less homogeneous than generally taken for granted, and that subtle diffferences in meaning are involved, which limit the interchangeability. The other two parameters confirm this conclusion.

Ad (iii): example (13e) exhibits a use of parenthetical *credo* for which I have found no parallels of the other modalizing verba sentiendi. Another instance is (14):

(14) Sed quia qui mecum sunt, credo (?? (ut) puto/opinor/existimo/arbitror/sentio) quod maestitiam meam non ferunt, domum properant, ... proficiscar hinc (Cic. *Att.* 13.26.2)

---

11. I treat the two expressions as equivalent here. See Pinkster (1987) on the emphatic character of the presence of the personal pronoun.

'But because those who are with me, I suppose because they cannot put up with my melancholy, are in a hurry to go home, ... I shall leave here'

A number (6=25%) of the 24 instances of parenthetical *credo* in Cicero's letters introduce a causal satellite clause (which itself is added to another clause in a parenthetical way), whereas none of the other expressions occur in that way. Again this tendency seems to be detectable in other authors (e.g. Seneca *Epistulae*, Petronius and Apuleius).[12]

Finally, ad (iv): as to be expected, in view of the fact that the predicates under consideration always govern Declarative complements, the host clauses in which they are inserted parenthetically are always Declarative (including irrealis and potentialis cases, which I view as Declaratives as well), with one exception, namely *opinor*. This verb occurs in 'adhortative' host clauses as well, i.e. in clauses with a subjunctive mood verb which have a Directive illocutionary force (in 5 of the 48 instances in my sample). I have not seen instances of *opinor* modalizing (Directive) imperative mood host clauses. Instances of parenthetical *opinor* in Directive subjunctive mood clauses are (13b) and (4b) above, both with first person plural Agents.[13] However, when used as a main verb, *opinari* requires Declarative complements, just like the other mental state verbs under consideration. One conclusion arising from this, is that there is no complete parallellism between the properties of *opinor* as a matrix verb of a sentential complement and its use as a parenthetical modalizer, and that it is consequently impossible to derive the latter use from the former.[14] It is remarkable that in all cases in which *opinor* parenthetically accompanies Directive clauses, it happens to lack introductory *ut*, although on the whole in Declarative host clauses it relatively more frequently occurs with *ut* than without it. Whether or not *ut* is actually excluded in cases such as (4b) and (13b), the fact that it is lacking might be an indication that solitary *opinor* has a more particle like status than when it is subordinated, and that for this reason its use is extended to a wider range of clauses.

---

12. Plautus, Terentius, Petronius and Apuleius provide further instances of parenthetical *credo*, but none of the other mental state verbs, used with scope over causal clauses and causal prepositional phrases (e.g. with *propter* 'because of'), with purpose clauses, with participles indicating somebody's motives (such as *metuens* 'fearing' etc.) and with relative clauses with a so-called 'final' flavour. In Sen. *Ep.* 83.15.1 an exceptional case of *puto* precedes a *quia* clause, but the scope of *puto* seems to be the whole complex clause rather than the causal clause by itself (see Bolkestein 1998).
13. Elsewhere (Cic. *Mur.* 30) I found instances with first person singular Agents as well. In some contexts one might hesitate as to interpreting such instances as being a potentialis subjunctive mood rather than a (speaker-including) Directive; in other cases the adhortative force is clear.
14. I am not going into the verb *censeo* 'I judge, propose' here. All of the potential cases of parenthetical use of this verb allow of a main verb interpretation as well. In Bolkestein (1998) I show that, if they can be interpreted as parenthetical at all, there is no parallellism between its range of possibilities as a main verb and its use as a parenthetical verb.

The above findings show, first, that the behaviour of the category of modalizing verba sentiendi differs in several respects from parenthetical full clauses, and, second, that they themselves form a heterogeneous group, with differences in distribution which can perhaps be related to other semantic differences (for some further data see Bolkestein 1998).

4. Concluding remarks

In this paper I have argued that an investigation of parenthetical expressions in classical Latin should distinguish between various subcategories of parenthesis. The two types examined are parenthetical full clauses and parenthetical modalizing mental state verbs. These two categories show clear differences in behaviour. Parenthetical full clauses turn out to be sensitive to the pragmatic function distribution in the host clause: whether or not they occur at a syntactic break, they always occur before the main Focus of the sentence as a whole. They may therefore be viewed as a sort of 'floor-holding' device. They rarely occur within NP's, and if they do, the condition just stated still holds: there will, in that case, be a contrast between two attributes, one before and one (the strongest) after the parenthesis. Parenthetical modalizing mental state verbs, on the other hand, are not sensitive to the pragmatic function distribution of the host clause as a whole. They may follow the main Focus as well as precede it. They are also more frequent within NP's, and do not, in that case, require a contrast between elements on both sides of the parenthesis. In these respects they do indeed resemble modal adverbs. However, as a group they do not form a homogeneous category: they manifest differences in behaviour with respect to several parameters, such as the absence or presence of a subordinator, presence or absence of the emphatic personal pronoun *ego* or the particle *equidem,* the type of unit under scope, and the basic illocutionary force or sentence type of their host. For at least one of them, *opinor,* there is no complete parallelism between its use as a main, complement governing verb and its parenthetical use. This means that the two uses are less closely related than is suggested in some analyses.

Bibliography

Albrecht, M. von
  1964 *Die Parenthese in Ovids Metamorphosen und ihr dichterische Funktion.*
        Hildesheim: Olms
Bolkestein, A.M.
  1994 Participant tracking in Latin discourse. In: J. Herman (ed.) *Linguistic Studies*
        on Latin. Amsterdam/Philadelphia: Benjamins, p. 283-302
  1996 Is *'qui' 'et is'?* On the so-called free relative connection in Latin. In: H. Rosén
        (ed.) *Aspects of Latin. Papers from the Seventh International Colloquium on*
        Latin Linguistics. Innsbruck: Innsbrucker Beiträge zur Sprachwissenschaft,
        p. 553-566
  1998 Modalizing one's message in Latin: 'Parenthetical' verba sentiendi. In:
        Ch.-M. Ternes & D. Longrée (eds) *Oratio soluta — oratio numerosa: Les*
        mécanismes linguistiques de cohésion et de rupture dans la prose latine. Actes des
        huitièmes "Rencontres Scientifiques de Luxembourg", 1995. Études Luxembour-
        geoises d'Histoire & de Littérature Romaines, vol. 1, p. 22-33
Brandt, M.
  1994 Subordination und Parenthese als Mittel der Informationsstrukturierung in
        Texten. *Sprache und Pragmatik* 32, 1-37
Dik, S.C.
  1989 *The Theory of Functional Grammar.* Dordrecht: Foris (now: Berlin, Mouton
        De Gruyter)
Espinal, M.T.
  1991 The representation of disjunct constituents. *Language* 67, 726-762
Hofmann, J.B.
  1951³ *Lateinische Umgangssprache.* Heidelberg: Winter
Jong, J.R. de
  1986 Hyperbaton en informatiestruktuur. *Lampas* 19, 323-331
Kroon, C.H.M.
  1995 *Discourse Particles in Latin: A Study of* nam, enim, autem, vero *and* at.
        Amsterdam: Gieben
Matthiessen, C. & S.A. Thompson
  1988 The structure of discourse and subordination. In: Haiman, J. & S.A. Thomp-
        son (eds) *Clause Combining in Grammar and Discourse.* Amsterdam/Phila-
        delphia: Benjamins, p. 275-329
Pinkster, H.
  1987 The pragmatic motivation for the use of subject pronouns : the case of
        Petronius. In: Mellet, S. (ed.) *Études de linguistique générale et de linguistique*
        latine offertes en hommage à Guy Serbat. Paris: Société pour l'Information
        Grammaticale, p. 369-379
  1990 *Latin Syntax and Semantics.* London/New York: Routledge
Pittner, K.
  1995 Zur Syntax von Parenthesen. *Linguistische Berichte* 156, 85-108

Risselada, R.

    1989 Latin illocutionary parentheticals. In: Lavency, M. & D. Longrée (eds) *Actes du cinquième Colloque de Linguistique Latine*. Cahiers de l'Institut de Linguistique de Louvain 15, 367-78

Roschatt, A.

    1883 *Über den Gebrauch der Parenthese in Cicero's Reden und rhetorischen Schriften.* Erlangen: Gymnasium Program

Ziv, Y.

    1985 Parentheticals and Functional Grammar. In: Bolkestein, A. M., C. de Groot & J.L. Mackenzie (eds) *Syntax and Pragmatics in Functional Grammar.* Dordrecht: Foris (now: Berlin, Mouton De Gruyter), p. 181-191

Deictic and (pseudo-)anaphoric functions of the pronoun *iste*

Jan R. de Jong

This paper deals with the functions of iste *as compared with the other demonstrative pronouns and the anaphoric pronoun* is. *Unlike several recent proposals that take a more radically pragmatic line, the approach taken here is in line with the essentially semantic theory of personal deixis, as set out e.g. by Bach (1891), according to which the three demonstratives* hic, iste, *and* ille *are systematically connected with the three grammatical persons. Because, however, the present paper is based on a more sophisticated view of deixis, which distinguishes e.g. between 'local' and 'textual' deixis, there is more room to account for the variation that we actually find in Latin texts. There are many contexts in which more than one demonstrative would be appropriate; but there are some in which just one pronoun is appropriate, and these contexts that tell us most about the true nature of that pronoun. Because* iste *occupies an extreme position on the Speaker-Addressee dimension, it is there that we have to look for its most 'typical' functions. The paper therefore mainly deals with the use of* iste *in Plautus. At the end of the paper the conclusions based on comedy are tested in a non-dialogic text, viz. Seneca.*

0. Introduction

The goal of this paper is to discuss various functions of the pronoun *iste*, especially in Plautus, by comparing its usage with that of the other demonstratives and the anaphoric pronoun *is*. It is a sequel to De Jong (1996), in which I dealt with the borderline between deixis and anaphora. There, I arrived at the conclusion that demonstrative pronouns, when referring to context or items mentioned in the context, perform a function that is essentially different from that of anaphoric pronouns, even if both may sometimes be used under the same circumstances. Demonstratives always refer to entities in extra-linguistic reality, whereas anaphora involves reference to intra-linguistic entities. Text uttered by some speaker becomes part of the extra-linguistic reality and hence may be referred to by deictic means. I proposed the term textual deixis[1] for this type of reference in order to distinguish it from anaphora proper.

In the earlier paper I showed that distributional differences in Caesar between the pronoun *is* and the demonstratives *hic* and *ille* can be accounted for by the differing modes of reference in each case. Due to the nature of the text I did not have the opportunity to deal with the pronoun *iste*, which occurs infrequently in

---

1. I use the term in a broader sense than Lyons (1977: 667).

the type of text concerned. In order to study the role of *iste* in textual deixis, the natural starting point is Plautus and Terence.

The most important, and most influential, study of *iste* and demonstratives in general in the Early Latin is Bach (1891). Bach's views have found their way into our grammars and commentaries and seem to be widely accepted. They are the classical formulation of the theory of personal deixis, which says that the three demonstratives are systematically connected with the three grammatical persons. It is remarkable that later studies of Latin demonstratives, such as Keller (1946), Kurzová-Jedličková (1961) and Fontan (1965), reject Bach's theory wholly or in important respects. Ehlers' *TLL* article, however, analyses *iste* along more traditional lines.

More recently, Bolkestein and Van de Grift (1995) proposed a set of rules determining the selection of referential devices in narrative discourse. This rule system in their view is, as far as demonstratives are concerned, separated from the spatio-temporal usage of the same devices. In this view the textual functions of *hic* and *ille* are completely detached from their meaning as first and third person demonstratives. The pronoun *iste* does not have a place in this system.

In this paper I will defend Bach's theory of personal deixis, but I will take a minimalist rather than Bach's maximalist stand, which holds that, in each context, there is just one appropriate pronoun. Instead, I will argue that there are many contexts where more than one pronoun would be fitting, but also that each of the demonstratives has a sort of core usage: a category of contexts where they cannot be replaced by another pronoun. It is these contexts that reveal most about the position of the pronoun within the demonstrative system as a whole.

In three part demonstrative systems it is the function of the middle term that enables one to tell a person-based system apart from a system based on proximity relations (Anderson & Keenan 1985), since the distributional properties of proximate and first person demonstrative pronouns are very similar, and the same holds for distal and third person demonstratives. Therefore, an analysis of *iste* is essential to the analysis of the Latin demonstrative system as a whole.

1. Interpretation of demonstrative variability in Plautus

In Plautus we find at least three types of pronominal deixis. The two most common types are exemplified in (1) and (2). (1) is a clear case of local deixis with the Speaker, we may assume, pointing his finger at the designated person. (2) on the other hand, is an instance of textual deixis; the act of deixis is directed at the *text* containing a referring expression, not at the location where the referent is situated: the Speaker does not point at the horizon in the direction of Piraeus.

(1)   (...) atque in *hunc* intende digitum: *hic* leno est (Pl. *Ps.* 1144)
       'he's the man to point the finger of scorn at: he's the pimp'

(2)   Strenue
       curre in Piraeum, atque unum curriculum face.
       Videbis iam *illic* navem qua advecti sumus. (Pl. *Trin.* 1102-1104)
       'Quick, run down to Piraeus, and make one long run of it! The ship we
       came in is there now, you'll see it.'

Of course, it is not always possible to make clear a distinction between the two
types. The first instance of *ille* in (3) must be a case of local deixis, as for the
following two instances we cannot be so sure; they could be interpreted as repeated
instances of local deixis, or, perhaps more plausibly, as textual deixis:

(3)   Sed Amphitruonis *illic* est servos Sosia:
       a portu *illic* nunc cum lanterna advenit.
       Abigam iam ego *illum* advenientem ab aedibus. (Pl. *Am.* 148-150)
       'But there is Amphitryon's servant Sosia — just coming from the harbour
       with a lantern. I'll bustle him away from the house as soon as he gets here.'

At least one more type of deixis should be distinguished, as cases such as the
following fit in neither with the local nor with the textual deixis type. This is
often the case when the demonstrative is used as a preparative pronoun:[2]

(4)   Ego sum *ille* Amphitruo, cui est servos Sosia (Pl. *Am.* 861)
       'I am that Amphitryon who has a servant Sosia'

Just as for Caesar, the material in Plautus also begs the question of the borderline
between textual deixis, such as in (2), and anaphora proper, such as in (5):

(5)   (...) ibo ad medicum atque *ibi* me toxico morti dabo (Pl. *Mer.* 472)
       'I'll go to a doctor and end it all [there] with poison'

In the present paper I shall only address this question when dealing with *istuc* and
id when used with cross-speaker boundary reference .
       Examples such as (6) below are adduced by Keller (1946) as evidence against
Bach's theory of personal deixis. This example, as well as a number of others like

---

2. Example (27) below is another example of this type of deixis without a relative clause.

it (three of which we will deal with later on), are from monologues. In (6) Diniarchus has taken leave of his beloved Phronesium and starts to sing her praise. All three demonstratives are used with reference to the girl, and Keller regards this as evidence against the hypothesis of personal deixis.

(6)   Vale.
    pro di immortales, non amantis mulieris,
    sed sociae unanimantis, fidentis fuit   435
    officium facere quod modo *haec* fecit mihi,
    suppositionem pueri quae mihi credidit,
    germanae quod sorori non credit soror.
    ostendit sese iam mihi medullitus:
    scio mi infidelem numquam, dum vivat, fore.   440
    egone *illam* ut non amem? egone *illi* ut non bene velim?
    me potius non amabo quam *huic* desit amor.
    ego *isti* non munus mittam? iam modo ex hoc loco
    iubebo ad *istam* quinque deferri minas,
    praeterea obsonari <una> dumtaxat mina.   445
    multo *illi* potius bene erit quae bene volt mihi,
    quam mihi, qui mihimet omnia facio mala. (Pl. *Truc.* 433-447)
'And you! Ye immortal gods! She's more than my loving girl, she's my mutual-hearted, trustful little pal to treat me as she treated me just now and confide the substitution of that child to me, a thing no sister would confide to her own sister. Now she has opened up her very inmost thoughts to me. She'll never in all her life be faithless with me, I know that. Ah, and I, shouldn't I love her? Shouldn't I wish her everything that's good? I'll cease to love myself rather than fail in love for her. I not send her some present? I'll go this very instant and have twenty-five pounds brought over to her, yes, and at least another fiver's worth of edibles. I'd rather make things nice for a girl so nice to me, lots more than for myself that do myself nothing but damage.'

In this passage all three demonstratives are used with reference to the same entity, the girl Phronesium. How are we to explain this variation? First of all, each of the different types of deixis has its own rules for selecting a particular demonstrative. Secondly, it is not always clear which type of deixis a particular instance represents. E.g. in the case of *huic* in line 442, it is unclear whether this is a case of local deixis, just as the first *haec*, or a case of textual deixis, 'this girl I just mentioned'. The occurrences of the pronoun *ille* in this passage could very well be instances of textual deixis: as such they would not refer to Phronesium by way of direct local deixis ('that girl over there') but indirectly ('that girl I was speaking about'). The pronoun *ille* is often used in this way instead of *is*, especially, as twice in line 441, if juxtaposed with emphatic personal pronouns. In other words, since there may be different types of deixis involved, there is not necessarily a contradiction in the fact that both *hic* and *ille* are used in this passage with reference to the same person. Even if they were the same type of deixis, we should not be surprised to find some variation. All this means that it is futile to try to explain, in each and every instance, why one pronoun has been used and not another. All one can hope to attain is to show that an occurrence of some pronoun falls within the range of possible contexts for that pronoun.

In this respect two problems remain with regard to the passage quoted. Firstly, why is the first mention of Phronesium by means of *haec*, and not, since she is off-stage, by means of *illa*? This is clearly an area where the hypothesis of personal deixis is vulnerable. When taken literally, as Bach does, it implies that in a given constellation of participants and referents only one demonstrative would be available for reference to a particular entity by a particular Speaker. Now this is clearly an overstatement. Normally, people off-stage will be referred to by means of *ille*. Nothing, however, could prevent a character in Plautus or any other speaker to *pretend* as if the person referred to is present and therefore use a phrase such as 'this girl'. The speaker might even gesture towards the position where she was before she left the stage. Any theory that attempts to reduce demonstrative selection to purely physical dimensions can easily be proven wrong by examples such as these.

Another problem with this passage is the alternation between *ille* and *iste* as demonstratives for textual deixis. *Ille* is quite common as such, especially in contrastive contexts, such as the last occurrence of *ille* in line 446 of passage (6), or when used in juxtapositon with accented pronouns such as *ego* in line 441. In such contexts it is preferred over anaphoric *is*. The occurrences of *iste*, on the other hand, are problematic, since it is unclear how the referent Phronesium relates to the Addressee. In fact, the notion 'addressee' itself is problematic in the case of monologues such as the present one.[3]

Various conclusions have been drawn from this variability of demonstrative usage. Bach tries to hold on to an extreme, topographical version of the hypothesis of personal deixis; this implies that, whenever there is a change of demonstrative, this means that there has been a change in the location of Speaker or Addressee, or of the entity referred to. Keller shows that this leads to absurd consequences,

---

3. We should not even exclude the possibility that the author deliberately varies these pronouns in order to characterise Diniarchus' state of mind. It is, however, legitimate to ask whether the range of possible contexts for the pronoun *iste* includes passages such as the present one. In section 4 below an explanation for this type of usage of *iste* will be offered.

and proposes to abandon the personal deixis hypothesis altogether and to replace it with the hypothesis of levels of deictic force: the Latin demonstratives represent three levels of deictic force, viz. low, medium and high for *ille*, *hic* and *iste* respectively.[4] The notion of deictic force is vague enough to accommodate all sorts of demonstrative usage, but does little to solve the real problem, viz. explaining why different demonstratives are used under similar circumstances. Also, with the bathwater the child is thrown away, since despite all the variability, there are clearly cases where only one demonstrative will fit, for obvious semantic reasons. If, for example, in a comedy an actor refers to the play he is in, there is just one option:

(7)   Verum si voletis plausum fabulae *huic* (*illi, *isti) clarum dare,
       comissatum omnes venitote ad me ad annos sedecim. (Pl. *Rud.* 1421-1422)
       'But if you are willing to give this play your loud applause, all come and
       make a night of it with me — sixteen years from now.'

In general, if a speaker refers to the location or ambience (including points in time) he finds himself in, he can only use the first person demonstrative. From Keller's point of view it is difficult to see why, in such contexts, just one level of deictic force (medium) would be appropriate. The approach advocated here is: (a) there are many contexts in which more than one demonstrative would be appropriate: we should, therefore, not be surprised to find that the same object is referred to by the same speaker by means of different pronouns, and (b) there are some contexts in which just one pronoun is appropriate, and naturally it is these contexts that tell us most about the true nature of that pronoun. As we have seen, for *hic* there is clearly an area that bears out a strong connection between this pronoun and first person or proximate deixis. I think that for *iste* such an area also exists, but we should not go looking for it along the spatio-temporal dimension, where it does not occupy an extreme position, and rarely enters into contrastive relationships.

---

4. Curiously similar to Keller (1946), both in procedure and solution, is Kirsner (1979) dealing with Dutch demonstratives. On the basis of attested examples such as the following:
    Daarna ruimde ze de tafel af en trok haar jas aan. "Staat *die* jas gek bij *die* muts"
    vroeg ze.
    'Afterwards she cleared the table and put on het coat. "Does *this* coat look crazy
    with *this* hat?", she asked'
Kirsner rejects the proximate/distal hypothesis regarding Dutch demonstratives and instead suggests that *deze* signals 'high deixis' and *die* 'low deixis'. Note that the translation given is Kirsner's. Translating *die* (commonly regarded as the Dutch distal demonstrative) with *this* he suggests that the English demonstratives function differently from the Dutch.

Iste, however, does occupy an extreme position on the Speaker-Addressee dimension,[5] and it is there that we have to look for its most 'typical' functions.

2. The notion of textual deixis in Plautus

Demonstratives in general are often used with reference to text. In monologic texts *hic* and especially *ille* are used in this way; in dialogue, speakers often deictically refer to each others' utterances. When this occurs, they typically do not use *hic* or *ille*, but *iste*. It is this use of *iste* that is at the centre of its functionality. It is frequent (about half of all the instances of *iste* are of this type) and it is exclusive: there are virtually no instances of other demonstratives with a similar function. The only competition it allows is that of *is*. The following is just one example of a type we find scores of in Plautus:

(8)   AP: <Quis hoc> dicit factum? EP: Ego ita factum esse dico.
       PE: Scin tu *istuc?* (* illud) EP: Scio. (Pl. *Epid.* 206-207)
       'Who says so? # I — I say so. # You know that for a fact? # I do.'

What the Speaker refers to by means of *istuc* in this example is the Addressee's speech act. This speech act is specified explicitly in the following example, by means of the noun *condicio*:

(9)   EP: Quia perire solus nolo, te cupio perire mecum,
       benevolens cum benevolente. TH: Abi in malam rem maxumam a me
       cum *istac* condicione. (Pl. *Epid.* 77-79)
       'I dislike to sink alone and yearn to have you sink with me — two devoted friends together. # Leave me alone, and go to the devil along with that proposal of yours!'

Note that not just speech acts, but all sorts of acts on the part of the Addressee are open to reference by means of the pronoun *iste*. In the following example, Pisto-clerus' angry reaction to people banging on his door contains both a neuter pronoun and a phrase with a specifying noun:

---

5. The relevance of the Speaker-Hearer dimension in deictic systems has recently been stressed by e.g. Jones (1995) in reaction to ego-centric accounts of deixis in works such as Bühler (1934) and Lyons (1977; 1995).

(10)   PA: (...) heus, ecquis hic est? ecquis hoc aperit ostium?
        ecquis exit? PI: Quid *istuc*? quae *istaec* est pulsatio? (Pl. *Bac.* 582-583)
        'Hi! Anyone here? Anyone minding this door? Anyone coming? # What's
        all this? What do you mean by pounding so?'

On the other hand, there are also numerous examples in Plautus of people
referring to a third person's words, especially in asides. In such cases, *ille* is
virtually the only pronoun available.[6] Compare (11), an aside, with (12), a direct
answer:

(11)   ME: Immo est < quod satis est >, et di faciant ut siet
        plus plusque <et> istuc sospitent quod nunc habes.
        EV: *Illud* mihi verbum non placet 'quod nunc habes.'
        tam hoc scit me habere quam egomet. (Pl. *Aul.* 545-548)
        'Ah well, you've got enough, and heaven make it more and more, and bless
        you in what you have now. # 'What you have now!' I don't like that phrase!
        He knows I have this money just as well as I do!'

(12)   GR: Papae, divitias tu quidem habuisti luculentas.
        LA: Miserum *istuc* verbum et pessimum est, habuisse, et nihil habere. (Pl.
        Rud. 1320-1321)
        'Whew! You surely had a grand big pile! # That's a dismal word, the very
        worst of words, "had," when what you have is nothing.'

Ille is also used with reference to words not directed at the Speaker (Trachalio, who
overhears Ampelisca's complaint):

(13)   PA: (...) Sed nunc sese ut ferunt res fortunaeque nostrae,
        par moriri est. neque est melius morte in malis,
        rebus miseris. TR: Quid est? quae *illaec* oratiost? (Pl. *Rud.* 674-676)
        'But seeing how things are and how fate treats us, death is welcome.
        Desperate, distracted creatures can do nothing better than die. # Eh? What
        sort of language is that?'

Iste is also often used with reference to entities *mentioned* by the Addressee, i.e.
entities that have an existence independent from the text itself:

---

6. But see section 3 for an instance of *iste* used in an aside.

(14) CU: (...) Lyconem quaero trapezitam.
      LY: (...) sed *istum* quem tu quaeris ego sum. (Pl. *Curc.* 406-419)
      'I'm looking for Lyco, the banker # (...) however, I am the man you are
      looking for'

When the demonstrative refers to the Addressee's text, *iste* is the only demonstrative available. However, with entities *mentioned* by the Addressee there is more
choice. In (15) *illuc negoti* takes up the Wife's *istaec flagitia*: it seems as if
Menaechmus is willing to admit the existence of some kind of affair, while at the
same implying, by means of the pronoun *illuc*, that it is far removed from himself,
thus rejecting the implication present in his wife's *istaec*.

(15) MA: Clanculum te istaec flagitia facere censebas potis?
      ME: Quid *illuc* est, uxor, negoti? (Pl. *Men.* 605-606)
      'Did you think you could commit such outrages on the sly? # What do you
      mean by that, my dear?'

In general, *ille* can very well be used for continued reference to an item introduced
by means of *iste*, since, once introduced, the referent is no longer located
exclusively within the Addressee's text:

(16) CO: Nempe uxor rurist tua, quam dudum dixeras
      te odisse aeque atque anguis. † LY: Egone *istuc* dixi tibi?
      CO: Mihi quidem hercle. LY: Ita me amabit Iuppiter,
      uxor, ut ego *illud* numquam dixi. (Pl. *Mer.* 760-763)
      'Your wife's in the country, of course; I remember your saying a while ago
      you hated her like a snake. # I? I said that to you? # Yes to me, by gad. # So
      help me Heaven, my dear, I never said any such thing!'

Failure to distinguish between textual and local deixis has led to considerable
confusion. Cf. the following exchange:

(17) AR: (...) hic pone, hic *istam* colloca cruminam in collo plane.
      LE: Nolo ego te, qui erus sis, mihi onus *istuc* sustinere. (Pl. *As.* 657-658)
      'Put it here, hang that wallet here around my neck in plain sight. # Let my
      master bear such a load? No sir, not I.'

Here, it looks as if both interlocutors can refer to same object by means of the
same deictic procedure, and as such the passage would provide evidence against the
theory of person-related deixis. It is in fact construed as such by Keller (1946: 287).

It is, however, not impossible at all to interpret in such a way that both instances of *iste* can be interpreted as cases of second person deixis, provided we make the distinction between local deixis (*istam cruminam*: the wallet you are carrying) and textual deixis (*onus istuc*: the burden you propose to take over).[7]

For a better understanding of the nature of textual deixis, a comparison between *iste* and *is* is also instructive. In (18) and (19) we find *iste* referring to entities mentioned by the Addressee. This is also the area where the competition between *iste* and *is* starts.

(18)   ME: Cui, malum, parasito? certo haec mulier non sanast satis.
       ER: Peniculo. ME: Quis *iste* est Peniculus? qui extergentur baxeae? (Pl. *Men.*
       390-391)
       'What parasite, confound it? There's certainly something wrong with the
       woman's wits. # Brush, I mean. # What brush is that? One you clean your
       shoes with?'

(19)   PE: (...) ei, pallam refer.
       ME: Quae *istaec* palla est? (Pl. *Men.* 618-619)
       'go, bring back the mantle. # Mantle? What mantle?'

In (18) Menaechmus's question is directed more at the name of Peniculus (and therefore at the Addressee's *text*), than at his identity, so the choice for the demonstrative is understandable. The procedure of textual deixis is also used here in order to reject the presupposition of existence of the referent of *Peniculus*. The same holds for *istaec* in (19). Here it is Menaechmus's strategy to deny the existence of a mantle such as Peniculus mentions. Again there is an element of rejection in the use of *iste* here. Note that this use of *iste* is closely connected with the so-called derogatory function of *iste* (see section 3 below). In (20), on the other hand, Menaechmus jokingly pretends to accept the existence of a certain Menaechmus other than he, and asks about this person's identity, using *is*. His wife, however, rejecting this person's existence, uses *istic* ('that person is no one else than you'). In (21) *Ubi is est* is a more sincere counterpart to Menaechmus's question in (20).

(20)   ME: Quis *is* homo est? MA: Menaechmus quidam. ME: (...)
       quis *is* Menaechmust? MA: Tu *istic*, inquam. ME: Egone? MA: Tu.
       (Pl. *Men.* 650-651)

---

7. Later in the same exchange the same speaker uses *hic* to refer to the same object (*hanc* in line 662).

'Who is this man? # A certain Menaechmus. # ... Who is this Menaechmus?
You yourself, I tell you. # I? # You.'

(21)   EP: Aggrediar hominem. Advenientem peregre erum [suom] Stratippoclem
      impertit salute servos Epidicus. ST: Vbi *is* est? EP: Adest. (Pl. *Epid.* 126-127)
      'I'll go to him. To master Stratippocles returning form abroad best wishes
      are extended by servant Epidicus, sir. # Epidicus? Where? # Present.'

When we compare neuter substantival *istuc* and *id* we find that, predominantly, *id*
refers to precisely identifiable constituents (*quae loquerentur* in 22, *meam rem agere*
in 23 and *quod plurimi exoptant sibi* in 24). *Istuc*, on the other hand, often has a
more vague reference: to sentences or utterances as a whole (cf. 25-26).

(22)   PE: Occepere aliae mulieres
   duae post me sic fabulari (...)
   nec satis exaudibam, nec sermonis fallebar tamen,
   quae loquerentur. PE: *Id* lubidost scire. (Pl. *Epid.* 236-240)
   'Two other women began chattering behind me, so, I drew away a bit
   purposely, pretended not to notice their conversation; I couldn't catch all
   they said, but not much escaped me, just the same. # I should very much like
   to know what it was.'

(23)   PH: Hoc prius volo,
   meam rem agere. TH: Quid *id* est? PH: Vt mihi hanc despondeas. (Pl. *Cur.*
   670-671)
   'But first I want to settle my own affair. # What is that? # That you promise
   me your sister.'

(24)   CH: (...) tibi optigit quod plurimi exoptant sibi.
     LA: Quid *id* est? CH: Vt id quod quaerant inveniant sibi. (Pl. *Rud.* 873-874)
     'You've obtained what most people pray for. # What's that? # To get what
     suits them.'

(25)   IU: (...) mihi necesse est ire hinc; verum quod erit natum tollito.
     AL: Quid *istuc* est, mi vir, negoti, quod tu tam subito domo
   abeas? (Pl. *Am.* 501-503)
   'I am obliged to leave you — but don't expose the child. # Why, my
   husband, what is it takes you away so suddenly?'

(26) MN: (...) Pistoclere, perdidisti me sodalem funditus.
      PI: Quid *istuc* est? MN: Quid est? Misine ego ad te ex Epheso epistulam
      super amica, ut mi invenires? (Pl. *Bac.* 560-562)
      'Pistoclerus, you have ruined me, your chum, ruined me utterly. # Eh?
      What's that? # What's that? Didn't I send you a letter from Ephesus about
      my mistress, asking you to find her for me?'

Again, we find that the demonstrative is used with reference, however vague, to
entities in extralinguistic reality: utterances, (speech) acts and attitudes of the
Addressee.

3. 'Derogatory' function of iste

A few words are in order about the so-called 'derogatory' function of *iste*. Some
deny (Bach and Keller in particular) that *iste* in early Latin can have this function,
with the argument that *hic* and *ille* can be used in derogatory contexts as well.
Although this is true, it is not entirely the point; the question should be: are there
any instances with *iste* where no other factor except the derogatory function could
explain the choice of the pronoun. I think there are, e.g. (27), a nice minimal pair:

(27) (...) nam *istos* reges ceteros
      memorare nolo, hominum mendicabula:
      ego sum *ille* rex Philippus. o lepidum diem. (Pl. *Aul.* 702-704)
      'As for the rest of your big kings — not worth mentioning, poor beggarlets!
      I am the great King Philip. Oh, this is a grand day!'

Contrary to first and third person demonstratives, *iste* acquiring a derogatory
function seems such a likely development for a second person demonstrative[8] (it
is only a small step from 'association with the Addressee' to 'non-association with
the Speaker') that it is implausible that this derogatory function of *iste* should at
any period have been unavailable. This function could easily have developed from
the category of textual deixis, where there is often a derogatory shade of meaning
present:

(28) LY: (...) OL: Nugae sunt *istae* magnae. (Pl. *Cas.* 333)
      'That's all rubbish'

---

8. The same phenomenon can be observed in Spanish, where the second person demonstrative *ese*
also has a secondary, derogative, meaning (Hottenroth 1982: 148).

(29) (about the *erilis noster filius* mentioned by the Addressee) ego *istunc* non novi adulescentem vostrum. (Pl. *Truc.* 302)
'as for that young man of yours, I don't know him'

The derogatory function of *iste* could also account for instances such as the following:

(30) Actutum fortunae solent mutari, varia vitast:
nos divitem *istum* meminimus atque *iste* pauperes nos: (Pl. *Truc.* 219-220)
'Fortunes keep changing round, all in a wink, life takes such turns. We remember him as rich, and he remembers us as poor:'

The passage is a true soliloquy (*tandem sola sum*, line 211), so that there can be no association with the Addressee. The contempt expressed by derogatory *iste*, however entirely fits the context: cf. *odium meum* in line 210 referring to the same person.

4. Discussion

We have established so far that in dialogue *iste* is the preferred pronoun when reference is made to an utterance of the Addressee and that this is the area where the nature of *iste* as a second person demonstrative manifests itself most clearly.

I now return to instances of *iste* in what, at least superficially, seems to be a monologic context. (31) and (32) are examples of this type. In (31) *istaec* refers to Peniculus' earlier statement: in order to keep a person from running away it's best to give him plenty to eat. In (32) the Speaker tells the audience about his girlfriend and how he wants his neighbour to hire a house for her.

(31) PE: (...) Apud mensam plenam homini rostrum deliges;
dum tu illi quod edit et quod potet praebeas,   90
suo arbitratu adfatim cottidie,
numquam edepol fugiet, tam etsi capital fecerit,
facile adservabis, dum eo vinclo vincies.
Ita *istaec* nimis lenta vincla sunt escaria: (Pl. *Men.* 89-94)
'A loaded table — tie his snout to that! Just you deal him out meat and drink to suit his pleasure and his appetite each day, and he'll never run — Lord, no! — no matter if he's done a deed for hanging. You'll keep him easily so long as you bind him with these bonds. They're such extraordinarily tenacious bonds, these belly-bands:'

(32)   (...) uxor me exspectat iam dudum esuriens domi;
       iam iurgio enicabit, si intro rediero.
       Verum hercle postremo, utut est, non ibo tamen,
       sed hunc vicinum prius conveniam quam domum
       redeam; ut mihi aedis aliquas conducat volo,   560
       ubi habitet *istaec* mulier. Atque eccum it foras. (Pl. *Mer.* 557-561)
       'my wife has been hungrily awaiting me there this long while. Her tongue
       will do me to death in no time, once I'm back inside. But just the same, I
       tell you what, by Jove, for all that I'm — not going in. No, I'll see my
       neighbour here before I go back home: I want him to hire some house for
       me, for that girl to live in. Aha! There he is, coming out!'

The value of *iste* in instances such as these is something like 'the X I have been
telling you about'. It appears to be a means of involving the audience in the mock-
conspiratory atmosphere present in these passages: the Speaker lets the audience in
on a secret. The object which is central in this secret is referred to by means of *iste*.
Another similar means to achieve this type of mood appears to be the use of the
second person with a vague reference (*dum tu ... praebeas* etc. in example 31). In the
context of (32) we find the same phenomenon (*adulescens quom sis ... rei tuae
convenit operam dare*, lines 550-551). The occurrences of *iste* in passage (6), with
which we started our discussion, can be explained along the same lines. Here the
rhetorical questions are yet another means of involving the audience. Again *iste*
refers to the object that is central in Diniarchus' thoughts. The same mock-
conspiratory mood is also present in many of the prologues, such as (33) from the
Casina:

(33)   Nunc sibi uterque contra legiones parat,
       paterque filiusque, clam alter alterum:
       pater adlegavit vilicum, qui posceret
       sibi *istanc* uxorem: (...) (Pl. *Cas.* 50-53)
       'And now the pair of them, father and son, are mustering their opposing
       legions, each without the other's knowledge. The father has commissioned
       his bailiff to ask the girl in marriage:'

The audience has been told about the girl Casina, and about a father and a son
who are both in love with her; each of them wants his own slave to marry her *qui
posceret sibi instanc uxorem* 'so that he can love her for his won'. Note that this
type of reference, 'the X I've been telling you about' is especially helpful in
referentially over-crowded passages such as this one.

Occasionally this type of use of *iste*, strongly involving the Addressee, is also encountered in expository prose, such as the following passage from Cato:

(34)   nunc, uti cognoscas naturam earum, prima est levis quae nominatur ... et item est tertia, quae lenis vocatur, minutis caulibus, tenera, et acerrima omnium est *istarum*, tenui suco, vehementissima (Cato *Agr.* 157.2-3)
'to give, then, the several varieties: the first is the so-called smooth ... so also is the third, the mild, with small stalk, tender, and the most pungent of all'

Again we observe a strong involvement of the Addressee (*uti cognoscas*) in this passage. The same phenomenon, on a much larger scale, is found in Seneca. Seneca, it would seem, is the first author to deviate significantly from the classical pattern of pronominalisation.

The most striking aspect of the pronominal system in Seneca is the virtual disappearance of the pronoun *is*, except for two functions: in the genitive and as a preparative pronoun. *Is* in other functions has been largely replaced by *ille* and *iste*. Two examples of *iste* in this function can be observed in passage (35), on the subject of meteors:

(35)   Tunc ignes tenuissimi iter exile designant et caelo producunt. Ideo nulla sine eiusmodi spectaculis nox est; non enim opus est ad efficienda *ista* magno aeris motu. Denique, ut breviter dicam, eadem ratione fiunt *ista* qua fulmina, sed vi minore. (Sen. *Nat.* 1.1.6)
'Then the extenuated fires make a slender path and draw it out in the sky. So, no nights are without spectacles of this kind; for to produce them there is no need of great atmospheric movement. Finally, let me say it briefly, they are produced by the same cause as lightning bolts are but by less force.'

Here we find *ista* referring back twice to *eiusmodi spectaculis*. Again, as in Plautus, the question is: is *iste* here equal to *is* (or to *is* as it functions in other authors) and *ille* in Seneca? I think it is not. We should bear in mind that almost all of Seneca's work is highly interactional in nature. The author often speaks in the first person (as in *ut breviter dicam* in the example passage). The Addressee in all these works, in this case Lucilius, is tangibly present: questions are, for example, put in his mouth. Most likely, the prominence of *iste* in these texts has to do with this interactional nature, which implies the presence of the Addressee, the second person.

Iste in Seneca primarily refers to information already communicated to the Addressee, to knowledge shared by Speaker and Addressee and to topics elaborated upon in the preceding context. Let us compare the use of *ille* and *iste* in the following passage, from the same general context as the preceding one:

(36)   Illud enim stultissimum, existimare aut decidere stellas, aut transilire, aut aliquid illis auferri et abradi. Nam si hoc fuisset, etiam defuissent; nulla enim nox est qua non plurimae ire et in diversum videantur abduci. Atqui, quo solet, quaeque invenitur loco et magnitudo sua singulis constat; sequitur ergo ut infra *illas ista* nascuntur et cito intercidant quia sine fundamento et sede certa sunt. (Sen. *Nat.* 1.1.10)

'Yet it is the stupidest thing to suppose that stars actually fall, or jump across, or that anything is taken or rubbed away from them. If this were so, the stars would have perished. Yet every night very many seem to fall and to be carried off in different directions. Still, each star is found in its usual place and its size remains constant. It follows therefore that the fires are produced below the stars and quickly collapse because they are without support and without fixed position.'

Here *illas* serves as the replacement for a plural *eas* referring to the most recent antecedent, the stars, whereas *ista* refers to the general topic of the discussion, which has already been elaborated upon and about which information has been communicated to the Addressee. We see that, due to the divergent nature of these texts, a function of the pronoun *iste* that was peripheral in Plautus has become the most prominent one in Seneca.

5. Conclusion

I draw some conclusions. Firstly, the status of *iste* as a second personal demonstrative is confirmed by the fact that, in Plautus, is the only demonstrative that can be used with reference to text produced by the Addressee. Secondly, there is a clear difference between *iste* used for textual deixis and *is* used for anaphora. Thirdly, at the periphery of textually deictic *iste* there is a group of instances where *iste* refers to information already communicated to the Addressee. Thus, while *ille* refers to common information with no implication concerning the source of that information, *iste* implies that the information was conveyed in the preceding communication. Fourthly, the same opposition appears to underlie the choice between *ille* and *iste* in Seneca, where both pronouns have gained more prominence due to the virtual disappearance of *is*. Fifthly, there is evidence that the so-called derogatory function of *iste* is an independent function of the pronoun, which cannot be reduced to a side-effect of one of its other functions.

Bibliography

Anderson, S.R. & E.L. Keenan
  1985 Deixis. In: T. Shopen (ed.) *Language Typology and Syntactic Description.* Cambridge: Cambridge University Press, vol. 3, p. 259-308
Bach, J.
  1891 De usu pronominum demonstrativorum apud priscos scriptores Latinos. In: W. Studemund (ed.) *Studien auf dem Gebiete des archaischen Lateins.* Berlin: Weidmann, vol. 2 p. 145-415
Bolkestein, A.M. & M. van de Grift
  1995 Participant tracking in Latin discourse. In: J. Herman (ed.) *Linguistic Studies on Latin.* Amsterdam/Philadelphia: Benjamins, p. 283-302
Bühler, K.
  1934 *Sprachtheorie.* Jena: Fischer
Fontan, A.
  1965 Historia y systemas de los demostrativos latinos. *Emerita* 33, 71-107
Hottenroth, P.-M.
  1982 The system of local deixis in Spanish. In J. Weissenborn & W. Klein (eds) *Here and There: Cross-linguistic Studies on Deixis and Demonstration.* Amsterdam/Philadelphia: Benjamins, p. 133-153
Jones, P.
  1995 Philosophical and theoretical issues in the study of deixis. A critique of the standard account. In: K. Green (ed.) *New Essays in Deixis: Discourse, Narrative, Literature.* Amsterdam/Atlanta: Rodopi, p. 27-48
Jong, J.R. de
  1996 The borderline between deixis and anaphora. In: H. Rosén (ed.) *Aspects of Latin. Papers from the Seventh International Colloquium on Latin Linguistics, Jerusalem 19-23 April 1993.* Innsbruck: Innsbrucker Beiträge zur Sprachwissenschaft, p. 499-509
Keller, R.M.
  1946 *iste deiktikon* in the early Roman dramatists. *Transactions of the American Philological Association* 77, 261-317
Kirsner, R.S.
  1979 Deixis in discourse: An exploratory quantitive study of the modern Dutch demonstrative ddjectives. In: T. Givón (ed.) *Syntax and Semantics, vol. 12: Discourse and Syntax.* New York: Academic Press, p. 355-375
Kurzová-Jedličková, H.
  1961 Die Demonstrativa im Vulgärlatein. *Acta Antiqua Acad. Scient. Hung.* 11, 121-143
Lyons, J.
  1977 *Semantics.* Cambridge: Cambridge University Press
  1995 *Linguistic Semantics.* Cambridge: Cambridge University Press

Discourse particles, tense, and the structure of Latin narrative texts

Caroline H.M. Kroon

Narrative texts are structured primarily on the basis of their thematic development, in which referent continuity, event continuity, and continuity of the time and place of action play an important coherence-creating role. In addition, narrative texts usually also display a 'rhetorical structure', which is not concerned with extralinguistic, content-based coherence, but rather with the way in which the narrator presents the content of his narrative. As such, it accounts for inter alia the alternation of main story-line events and additional material, and (on the main story-line) between prominently and less prominently presented events (phenomena which are all often referred to in terms of 'foreground' and 'background'). This article focuses mainly on linguistic devices in Latin that are used for signalling this rhetorical type of narrative structure. It discusses the role of a number of discourse particles in Latin narrative texts (at, autem, enim, ergo, igitur, nam, and vero) and explores the extent to which these particles correlate with particular narrative tenses. By doing so it attempts to gain more insight into (i) the functions of these particles in narrative texts, (ii) the discourse functions of the various narrative tenses, and (iii) the structure of narrative texts more in general. In this context contentious notions such as 'foreground' and 'background', and 'narration' and 'exposition' are discussed from a mainly linguistic viewpoint.

0. Introduction: narrative structure[1]

'Textual structure' is not an unequivocal term. When discussing, for instance, the structure of narrative texts, we have to be aware of the fact that such texts display several forms of structure, which may be subsumed under two general headings, *thematic structure* and *rhetorical structure*.

Thematic structure involves coherence of the content. From the perspective of content, narrative texts can be analyzed as an intricate network of thematic chains which are based on referent continuity, event continuity, and continuity of

---

1. I would like to thank Rodie Risselada for her valuable comments on an earlier version of this article. I have also gratefully profited from discussions with Jaap Wisse and Irene de Jong, and with various other people who were present at one of the oral presentations on which this article is based. Thanks are due also to Paula Rose and my students Josselijn Boessenkool and Annelie Volgers (seminar on Latin Linguistics, winter 1995), who helped me collect the data.

the time and place of action. The main linguistic device for signalling thematic structure is, accordingly, the mechanism of anaphoric reference, in the form of lexical repetitions, anaphoric pronouns, anaphoric adverbs, zero-anaphora, and the like. Thematic chains may also, of course, be concluded or temporarily interrupted, in order to give way to new thematic chains. Such breaks in the thematic structure may, in turn, be marked linguistically as well, for instance by the use of full nominal phrases instead of anaphoric pronouns, by particular word order devices (e.g. fronting of new discourse topics), or by the use of particular text structuring particles. In this article I will be concerned only marginally with the thematic type of narrative structure.

Secondly, narrative structure can be viewed from a rhetorical perspective. A rhetorical analysis does not so much pertain to the extralinguistic, content-based coherence, as to the way in which the narrator presents (or, with a stronger term, manipulates) the narrative content in accordance with his specific communicative goals. In essence a narrator may confine himself, in telling a story, to an objective, chronological account of the successive, constitutive events, without adding background comments and without distinguishing, for instance, between central and more marginal events (the school essay type of narrative: "*And then ... And then ... And then ...* "). Far more common, however, especially in written narrative, is a mode of presentation in which the narrator explicitly differentiates between narrative main lines and subsidiary material. Within the narrative main line itself, certain events may in turn be presented more prominently than other events. As far as the rhetorical structure of Latin narrative texts is concerned, an important role seems to be played, not only by certain 'discourse particles', but also, and especially, by the various historical tenses that are available in the language.

The present article concentrates on these last two linguistic devices (discourse particles and the use of tenses), with special attention to the question whether in narrative texts there is a correlation between the two. The more concrete question to be answered is, thus, whether for a specific group of particles with a 'discourse' potential we can establish a statistic preference for particular historical tenses in their immediate environment. Such a statistical research might corroborate, or — if necessary — adjust, current views on the discourse functions of both phenomena.

A further-reaching goal of this article is also to demonstrate that this type of research may yield more insight into the complex phenomenon of narrative structure in general, and that it can provide us with more concrete, linguistically based interpretations of such ill-defined notions as *narratio, expositio, foreground,* and *background*. As for Latin, the definitions of foreground and background, for instance, are usually based on the criterion Tense, while the functions of the various historical tenses are, in turn, defined by making use of the notions foreground and background. If we are able to demonstrate that there is a certain correlation between the Tense parameter and some other parameter[2] (for instance the use of particular discourse particles), we might overcome the risk of such a circularity.

In the following I first discuss, in section 1, the use of the various historical tenses in Latin narrative texts. In section 2 I give a brief impression of the functions of a number of frequently used Latin particles (viz. *at, autem, enim, ergo, igitur, nam*, and *vero*), confining myself to their use in narrative texts. This leads to a number of hypotheses with regard to preferred combinations of these particles with particular historical tenses. Section 3 contains an overview of the statistical data I gathered with regard to these combinations. In section 4 I present some preliminary conclusions from the statistical data. Section 5 discusses, by way of illustration, the distribution of tenses with the particle *nam*. This is followed, in section 6, by a more general conclusion and by some suggestions for further research.

1. Parameter 1: tenses and the structure of narrative texts

A brief, but very instructive account of the use of tenses in Latin narrative texts can be found in Pinkster (1990: 236-242). Elaborating on his 1983 article in *Aufstieg und Niedergang der römischen Welt*, Pinkster argues that the typical functions of the various historical tenses in narrative texts (perfect, imperfect, pluperfect and historic present) can be explained from the specific semantic values of these tenses within the two-dimensional tense system he assumes for Latin. In this system the perfect is described in terms of anteriority to the moment of speaking, the pluperfect in terms of anteriority to a moment in the past, the imperfect as indicating simultaneity with a certain moment in the past, and the historic present as indicating simultaneity with the moment of speaking.

In narrative texts these semantic values provide a basis for various *discourse functions*. This means that the perfect is used mainly for the neutral presentation

---

2. See Bolkestein (1991) for a study of the correlation between the use of tenses and main clause vs. subordinate clause status. On account of a number of complicating factors this study does not yield clear results with regard to the foreground/background problem.

of a next step on the main story-line: the perfect indicates, without more, that a particular event occurred before the moment of speaking/writing. The imperfect, indicating simultaneity of an event with a certain moment in the past, is highly suitable for providing 'background' material, i.e. all kinds of information that do not belong to the main story-line, but are 'valid' at the same moment in the past at which a certain main-line event takes place. In like manner the pluperfect, which also has its reference point in the past, is used most commonly as a background-tense. And finally, the semantic value of the present (simultaneity with the moment of speaking) may be exploited in narrative texts for presenting past events with the connotation of an eye-witness report.[3] Like the perfect, the historic present is predominantly used for events on the main story-line, the perfect commonly being the more neutral form of expression, while the present is more marked.[4]

A deliberate alternation of these tenses in a narrative text may create a certain form of what in the introduction above has been called 'rhetorical structure'. One might also speak of 'narrative relief'. On the one hand the main story-line (usually characterized by the perfect and historic present) alternates with 'background' material (commonly marked by the imperfect or pluperfect). Within the main story-line, on the other hand, the coexistence of a *neutral* main story-line tense (the perfect) and a *marked* one (the historic present) provides a possibility for presenting main-line events in a neutral or a more prominent way.[5]

In a study of actual narrative texts Pinkster's quite straightforward theory proves to be usable to a large extent. However, a complication is formed by the fact that the narrative in a strict sense usually alternates with elements that do not belong to the story proper but may nonetheless refer to past events as well (e.g. authorial comment). As will become clear later on, this is not an irrelevant factor for my correlation research. For this and other reasons I will make use of a more elaborate picture of the use of tenses in Latin narrative texts. This picture is summarized in figure 1:

---

3. It is especially with regard to the semantic value of the present in the Latin tense system that opinions differ. For an alternative approach cf. e.g. Serbat (1988). This alternative approach is also discussed by Pinkster (this volume).
4. This observation seems to hold for other languages as well. See esp. Fleischmann (1990).
5. For comparable observations, see e.g. Chausserie-Laprée (1969: 369-411), Rosén (1980), Wehr (1984), and Pinkster (this volume).

figure 1: narrative structure and the distribution of tenses (source: Kroon & Rose, 1996: 75)

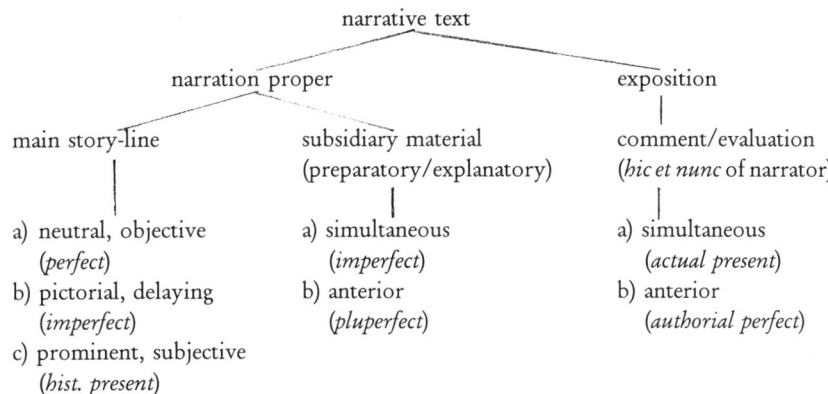

When viewed 'horizontally', narrative texts commonly consist of a narration proper (the *narratio*) and a number of intervening parts in which the narrator comments, so to speak, on what is being told (the *expositio*).[6] The narration proper concerns the whole of the events that make up the 'narrated world' as presented by the narrator. This 'narrated world' is usually situated in the past. At his own discretion the narrator may temporarily leave the narrated world for evaluating remarks or other forms of authorial comment on the narrated events, for procedural remarks relating to the process of narrating itself, or for a digression in which states of affairs are being described that do not (or not exclusively) belong to this specific narrated world. He then enters the *exposition*-layer of the text. Exposition-parts may be quite extensive, but may also be confined to a single remark. They are usually meant for adequately fitting the narrative proper into the here and now of the narrator and his audience, in accordance with the specific communicative goals of the narrator. We could also say that the exposition pertains to the communicative situation in which the narrative is conveyed, and that it is

---

6. The *narratio* is to a certain extent comparable to what Weinrich (1964) calls *erzählte Welt*, or Benveniste (1966: 237-250) *histoire*. Likewise the term *expositio* corresponds more or less to *besprochene Welt* or *discours*. For the use of the terms *narratio* and *expositio* in the context of Latin narrative, see e.g. Rosén (1980).

not so much a *constituent part of* the narrated world, as a *reflection on*, or *manipulation of*, the narrated world.[7]

In contrast to what one might perhaps conclude from figure 1, the narrator and the narrating situation are always present within the narration proper as well, although usually in a rather covert way. In situations in which the manifestation of the narrator is relatively explicit and overt, the borderline between narration proper and exposition may, however, become vague. Especially difficult to classify are, for instance, those sections in a text in which the narrator briefly preambles the essence of an immediately following episode, or in which he summarizes, in an epilogue manner, the story just told (cf. expressions like '*And the following unexpected events took place*'). Although sentences like these refer directly to the narrated world (to be) described, they are not themselves a constituent part of the chronological series of events that make up this world: they rather have a procedural function.[8] I therefore provisionally regards such text parts as a subcategory of exposition. Another solution might be to consider them a separate category in between narration proper and straightforward exposition.

The *narration proper* (left-hand part of figure 1) involves the presentation of two types of material a *main story-line* and what might be called *subsidiary material*. The main story-line (sometimes also called the 'foreground') consists of the successive events along which the narrative evolves. These main story-line events can be presented in at least three different ways or 'modes'.

a) First, they can be presented with hindsight from the *hic et nunc* of the narrator. The distance between the narrating and the narrated moment creates the impression of a neutral and relatively objective presentation of facts and may be exploited for a condensation of time. As stated above, this specific mode of presentation is in Latin usually characterized by the use of the perfect tense.

b) Main story-line events may be presented also in a more pictorial way, as if the narrator's camera is positioned in the narrated past itself and as if the events are told in their actual development. The Latin tense corresponding to this mode of presentation is the imperfect. The effect of the (relatively rare) use of the

---

7. In an attempt to give a definition of the term *narratio* (or *narration proper*) one could say that it applies to any stretch of text that is characterized by thematic unity and temporally sequenced clauses, referring to a narrated world that is marked out in time by a clear indication of its beginning and end. I intentionally avoid, in this section, the technical use of terms like *fabula*, *story* and *plot*, which in narratological theories have received various interpretations.
8. Equally difficult to classify are flashbacks and sections in which the narrator is running ahead of events that actually belong to a later stage in the narrative.

imperfect for main story-line events is a certain slowing down of the development of the narrative.[9]

c) Thirdly, main story-line events may be presented as if from the perspective of an eyewitness, who may be the main narrator (pretending that the narrating and the narrated event coincide) or one of the characters in the story. Whereas distance between narrating and narrated event usually yields the impression of an objective presentation of facts (cf. a. above), lack of distance seems to create the effect of 'subjectivity', 'expressivity' or 'vividness'. In Latin, as well as in many other languages, the characteristic tense associated with this mode of presentation is the historic present.[10] When used in alternation with the more 'detached' perfect tense, the historic present seems to be reserved for lending more prominence to main story-line events.[11] Unfortunately, we again find the term foreground used for this prominent rendering of events on the main story-line.[12] Since the term is used also for main story-line events in general (see my remark above), I will avoid any confusion and do not use the term at all in figure 1.

By subsidiary material (center column in figure 1) I mean those events *within the narrated world* which do not further the narrative in a chronological, sequential sense, but which serve as a preparation or support with regard to one or more main-line events. The Latin tenses most commonly involved in expressing this type of events are the imperfect and pluperfect. In the case of the imperfect the subsidiary event is represented as coinciding with some main-line event(s), in the case of the pluperfect it is indicated that the result of the subsidiary event is valid at the moment of occurrence of some main-line event(s). I avoid using the term 'background' here, for the very reason that this term tends to be used also for those parts of a narrative text which clearly belong to what I have called *exposition*. Because the difference between supportive material within the narrative proper (in figure 1 called 'subsidiary material') and supportive material outside the narrative

---

9. Indisputable examples of the use of the imperfect on the main story-line are those in which the imperfect is accompanied by typical 'main-line markers' such as *tum* (e.g. Verg. *A*. 6.3-4, cf. Stouthart, n.d.), *hinc, deinde, inde, repente*. The largest group of instances is however formed by imperfects that refer to iterative or distributive states of affairs (see also Rosén, 1980).

10. The historic present seems to share with the imperfect the feature of a pictorial presentation. This might explain why it is not totally excluded in 'background' passages.

11. It has been observed in the literature that in certain Latin narratives (Virgil's *Aeneis*, see Quinn 1968; Apuleius *Met.*, see Mellet 1984 and the reaction by Pinkster, this volume) the historic present seems to be used instead of the perfect as the more neutral, 'default' tense. Prominence might in such cases be achieved by other means (e.g. by the use of historic infinitives or other non-finite predicates).

12. See e.g. Wehr (1984).

proper (in figure 1 called 'exposition') might in theory be reflected by a difference in the tenses used, I wish, for the moment, to keep both concepts apart.

As typical exposition-tenses, finally, figure 1 mentions the actual present (to be distinguished from the historic present that typically belongs to the narration proper) and the authorial perfect (to be distinguished from the narrative perfect).[13] A typical example of the authorial use of the perfect is (1), to which I will return in section 5 below.

(1)   Augur in locum eius inauguratus Q. Fabius Maximus filius; in eiusdem locum pontifex — nam duo sacerdotia *habuit* — Ser. Sulpicius Galba. (Liv. 30.26.10)
       'In his place as augur his son Quintus Fabius Maximus was installed; likewise in his place as pontifex — for he held two priesthoods — Servius Sulpicius Galba.'

Summarizing thus far we can say that, mainly because of the steady alternation of narration proper and exposition parts, the distribution of tenses in Latin narrative texts is more complex than it might appear at first sight. Perfect, imperfect and present, for instance, all occur in more than one position in the diagram, and this is something to keep in mind while conducting a research of the type discussed in this article. At this point it is also necessary to emphasize that figure 1 is a somewhat artificial picture, which has been drawn up mainly for the purpose of conceptual and terminological clarity, and which does certainly not purport to capture all niceties of a narrative text.[14] As to the distribution of tenses, it does moreover not contain absolute rules, but only a number of clear tendencies.

One might have missed, in figure 1, a mention of the historic infinitive. Although this quite unique Latin phenomenon has been discussed extensively in the literature, until now there has been no real agreement as to whether the historic infinitive has a discourse function of its own, or has to be considered a stylistic variant of one of the finite narrative tenses. I will not elaborate on this

---

13. I use the terms 'narrative perfect' and 'authorial perfect' as a convenient shorthand for 'the use of the perfect within the narration proper' and 'the use of the perfect outside the narration proper', respectively, i.e. for two contextually different manifestations of a single tense and function. In fact it is essential to the theory discussed here that the 'narrative perfect' is considered as basically authorial (i.e. presenting past events with hindsight from the *hic et nunc* of the narrating situation).
14. An interesting further question would e.g. be how such narratological concepts as 'perspective' and 'focalisation' might correlate with the concepts distinguished in figure 1.

issue here myself, but refer to a recent article by Rosén (1995), in which the discussion is summarized. So much is clear, at any rate, that the historic infinitive typically occurs in the narration proper, and preferably on the main story-line. It is notable that it shares distributional properties with both the historic present and the imperfect: like the historic present the historic infinitive tends to occur in narrative climaxes with a strongly affective or expressive character; and like the imperfect it appears to be very much compatible with a decelerating mode of presentation, particularly in contexts involving states of affairs with an iterative or distributive character. If we would wish to locate the historic infinitive in figure 1, the best place would therefore probably be under b and c in the left-hand column.

2. Parameter 2: particles and the structure of narrative texts

In Kroon (1995) a number of Latin particles are described which have in common that they may somehow play a role in marking the structure of a text. They differ considerably, however, as to the specific ways in which this is achieved and as to the specific types of structure involved. Passing over many details, and concentrating mainly on the function of these particles in narrative texts,[15] I distinguish two main groups: one involving organization of the text, the other involving interaction management. This is summarized in figure 2:

figure 2: the particles studied (see Kroon 1995)

organization of the text	interaction management
autem, igitur, nam	at, enim, ergo, vero

The particles *autem, igitur* and *nam* are placed in the category 'organization of the text', on account of the fact that they mark, in a rather unambiguous way, the linking of two explicitly expressed text segments (of variable size).

The characteristic function of *autem*, not only in narrative texts but also in general, is the signalling of various forms of thematic discontinuity. It may occur,

15. The corpus on which the descriptions in Kroon (1995) are based comprises not only narrative texts, but also e.g. orations, philosophical prose and comedy.

for instance, at major boundaries in a text, i.e. at the transition of one major thematic chain to another. But it may also be used on a more local text level, to indicate a mere (discourse) topic shift or shift in perspective. A straightforward example from Latin narrative is (2), where *autem* is attached to a new discourse topic, thus emphasizing the beginning of a new stage in the description of the banquet at Trimalchio's house:

(2)   Petauristarii *autem* tandem venerunt. (Petr. 53.11)
       'But at last the acrobats came in.'

On account of the observation that *autem* is a typical marker of the thematic rather than of the rhetorical structure, it might be hypothesized that it has no specific preferences with regard to the Tense parameter.

Igitur and *nam*, on the other hand, are to be considered markers of the rhetorical structure of the narrative. In a certain respect they can be regarded as each other's opposites. The main function of *igitur* in narrative texts appears to be the marking of a transition to an important new event on the main story-line, which has been prepared by, or results from, the event(s) described in the preceding context.[16] On account of this function, it is to be expected that *igitur* occurs, in narrative texts, with typical main-line tenses as the perfect and historic present. *Nam*, on the other hand, usually signals a transition from the main story-line to a subsidiary text part with the function of explanation or elaboration. We therefore might expect *nam* to be highly compatible with a typical 'side-line' tense as the imperfect.[17] Examples of the typical use of *igitur* and *nam* in narrative texts are (3) and (4), respectively:

(3)   Multis contentionibus ... eo deducta est ut senatui permitterent. Patres *igitur*
       iurati ... censuerunt uti consules provincias inter se conpararent sortirenturve
       ... (Liv. 30.40.11-12)

---

16. *Igitur* is used also (though less frequently) for indicating a return to the narration proper after an exposition part. An example is Sal. *Jug.* 96, where after a digression on Sulla's life and character the narration proper is picked up by means of an *igitur*-clause. The structure of Sal. *Jug.* 95-96, and the role of particles in this structure, is discussed in Kroon (1995: 83-88). A comparable example is Cic. *de Orat.* 3.17.
17. For the expected compatibility of *igitur* with the perfect and *nam* with the imperfect see also Pinkster (1990: 237-38).

'After many disputes ... the decision was ultimately left to the senate. The senator therefore under oath ... decided that the consuls should determine their provinces by mutual agreement or by lot ...'

(4)   ... Hispanos ... presso gradu incedere iubet; ipse e dextro cornu — ibi *namque* praeerat — nuntium ad Silanum et Marcium mittit ut ... (Liv. 28.14.15)
'   ... he ordered the Spaniards ... to advance at a slow pace; from the right wing — for he was himself in command there — he sent a message to Silanus and Marcius that ...'

The particles in the right-hand column of figure 2 differ from those in the left-hand column in that they pertain, in one way or another, to the interaction process taking place between the narrator and his audience in the narrating situation. *At*, *enim* and *ergo* are not mere linkers of text segments, but have, so to speak, a certain 'interactional surplus-value'. *At*, for instance, usually occurs at thematic boundaries in narrative texts (just like *autem*), but in contrast to *autem* it indicates primarily that the narrator wishes to present the content of the text segment involved as surprising and as potentially contrary to the expectations of his audience at the particular moment. On account of this latter characteristic one might expect *at* to occur especially in combination with typical main-line tenses (the perfect, and perhaps also the more marked historic present and historic infinitive). A characteristic example of the use of *at* in narrative texts is (5). In the clause preceding *at* certain expectations have been built up (viz. that the enemy is about to thwart Caesar's troops), which are subsequently frustrated by the information conveyed in the *at*-clause:

(5)   Ipsi ex silvis rari propugnabant nostrosque intra munitiones ingredi prohibebant. *At* milites legionis septimae, testudine facta et aggere ad munitiones adiecto, locum ceperunt. (Caes. *Gal.* 5.9.6-7)
'The enemy came out of the woods to fight in small groups, and sought to prevent our troops from entering the fortifications. *But* the soldiers of the seventh legion formed a *tortoise* and threw up a ramp against the fortifications, and so took the position.'

Likewise *enim* has an interactional surplus-value as compared to for instance *nam*, with which it shares in narrative texts a considerable number of distributional properties. Both particles tend to occur in subsidiary text segments (rather than in segments containing main-line events), in the case of *enim* however with the added value of an appeal to consensus on the part of the audience. An example is (6), in which the appeal to consensus indicated by *enim* is apparently justified by the fact that the information conveyed in the *enim*-clause has been supplied already in the preceding context, as is evident from the addition *ut supra demonstratum est*:

(6)   Quae res (sc. tempestas) magnas difficultates exercitui Caesaris attulit. Castra *enim*, ut supra demonstratum est, cum essent inter flumina duo ... neutrum horum transiri poterat ... (Caes. *Civ.* 1.48.3)
        'This (i.e. the storm and the consequent breaking down of the bridges) caused serious difficulties to Caesar's army. For the camp being situated, as has been explained above (*ut supra demonstratum est*), between two rivers ... neither of these could be crossed ...'

Anyhow, on account of their preference for occurring with subsidiary material, one might expect both *nam* and *enim* to occur most frequently in combination with the imperfect and pluperfect.[18]

It is difficult to give a general indication of the function of *ergo* in narrative texts, not only because of its relatively rare occurrence in this type of texts, but also because of its quite uneven distribution.[19] In Kroon 1995 (92-93; 369-370) I argue that in general *ergo*, in contrast to its alleged synonym *igitur*, is used for signalling a reactivation of information that has been supplied earlier or that is easily inferrable (or follows automatically) from the preceding.[20] Accordingly, *ergo*-clauses often expand the discourse as it is, their main communicative point being the forestallment of a potential misunderstanding on the part of the reader/hearer. As such, *ergo* can be considered to play a certain role in the management of the interaction.

18. An other hypothesis might be that *enim*, by virtue of its 'interactional surplus-value', is more frequent in the exposition than in the narration proper (the interaction between a narrator and his audience is more likely to come to the surface in the exposition than in the strictly narrative parts).
19. In the narrative corpus I used for the present study (see section 3 below) *ergo* turned out to be by far the least frequent. The figures can be found in section 3, figure 4. Of the 78 *ergo*-instances as much as 35 were found in Petronius, 26 in Livy, 16 in Tacitus, 1 in Sallust, and none in Caesar.
20. In conversational texts we come across *ergo* particularly in requests for confirmation or verifying questions (or in related forms of repetitions of the content), in argumentative texts in statements that are already implied by (and therefore inferrable from) the immediately preceding context.

Although more research is needed here, I have the impression that this general, interactional function of *ergo* is to a certain extent also traceable in narrative texts. In a number of its occurrences it is found in combination with a recapitulative participle construction, which may count as inherently repetitive.[21] More or less comparable are cases in which *ergo* introduces a recapitulative summary of events described earlier. In a majority of cases, lastly, *ergo* appears to be used in much the same way as *igitur* (i.e. introducing a new stage in the development of the story), but with the interactional surplus-value of presenting the state of affairs referred to as matter-of-course (to be rendered by expressions like 'as could be expected').

An illustrative example is (7), in which *ergo* introduces a next step on the main story-line, which, however, is presented as an inevitable and logical conclusion based on various arguments, rather than as a mere next event in a series of causally related states of affairs. Livy is recounting a battle between Hannibal and the Roman praetor Fulvius near the Apulian town Herdonea. In the preceding sections he has been discussing at length the lack of discipline and recklesness of the Roman soldiers, the weakness of their commander, and the chaotic way in which the Roman lines have been drawn up. The situation on the Roman side is then unfavourably compared, in one brief but very powerful sentence (first sentence of the quotation in 7), to that of the enemy (*Et Hannibal ... aderat.*). The entire passage leaves no doubt as to the outcome of the battle, which finally follows in the *ergo*-clause.

(7)   (...) Et Hannibal haudquaquam similis dux neque simili exercitu neque ita instructo aderat. *Ergo* ne clamorem quidem atque impetum primum eorum Romani sustinuere. (Liv. 25.21.8)
     'And there was Hannibal, surely not that sort of a general, nor with that sort of an army, drawn up in that fashion. Consequently the Romans did not withstand even their shout and the first onset.'

As to the tenses used in *ergo*-clauses, one might e.g. predict a relatively high number of (authorial) perfects, and a relatively low number of imperfects and pluperfects.

Vero, finally, forms a class of its own, because its behaviour differs considerably from that of the other particles mentioned here, not only in narrative

---

21. Examples from my corpus are e.g. Petr. 21.6; 34.8; 73.5; 82.4.

texts, but also more in general. It has the characteristics of a modal particle rather than of a connective particle. This appears for instance from the fact that it is not confined to main clauses, and that it is often difficult to establish the precise scope of the particle. Especially relevant for the present study, however, is the observation that *vero* tends to occur in narrative segments which contain a surprising event, sudden turn, or climax. It emphasizes, in such contexts, that the narrator himself lends his authority to what is being told, regardless of how remarkable or unexpected the information may sound. *Vero* may therefore be considered an interactional rather than a strictly text structuring particle.[22] Example (8) may count as a representative instance:

(8)   (following an inserted speech)
       Tum *vero* tantus est clamor exortus ut hostes e castris exciret. (Liv. 10.19.12)
       'Then in truth they cheered so loud that the enemy were drawn out from
       their camp.'

On account of its specific function *vero* may be expected to occur predominantly with main-line tenses, and especially often with main-line tenses that indicate a certain prominence (i.e. the historic present and historic infinitive).

The hypotheses formulated in this section can be summarized as follows:
(i)   *autem* has no statistical preferences with regard to the tenses used in its
        immediate environment;
(ii)   *nam* and *enim* are relatively often combined with typical side-line tenses
        (imperfect and pluperfect);
(iii)   *igitur, at, ergo* and *vero* are relatively often combined with typical main-line
        tenses (perfect, historic present, historic infinitive);
(iv)   *vero* and perhaps also *at* are used more often with the historic present and
        historic infinitive than the other particles.

---

22. *Vero* can at the most be regarded as an *indirectly* organizing particle: in combination with other devices *vero* may contribute to an affective mode of presentation, which, in turn, may suggest a certain degree of prominence in the narration. The alternation of a neutral and a more affective narrative mode (in Kroon 1995: 322 referred to as a *chiaroscuro* technique) can be considered a specific form of what in the introductory section has been referred to as 'rhetorical structure'.

3. Corpus and statistical data

The hypotheses formulated above have been checked in a narrative corpus consisting of the following texts:[23]

corpus:
Caesar: *Gal.*; *Civ.* I
Sallust: *Cat.*; *Jug.*
Livy: I-X; XXI-XXX
Tacitus: *Ann.* XIII-XV; *Hist.* I-II
Petronius: *Sat.*

In this corpus I registered all instances of the particles involved, confining myself to main clauses in the indicative mood. Instances of these particles in direct or indirect speech were filtered out and only counted, the results of which are listed in figure 3:

figure 3: occurrence of the particles in (in)direct speech

	number of occurrences in (in)direct speech	% of all occurrences in the corpus
at	62	29%
autem	76	33%
enim	211	45%
ergo	67	46%
igitur	47	19%
nam	134	22%
vero	58	34%

Although not particularly relevant for the present study, these figures are quite interesting in themselves. They show, for instance, that in narrative texts particles

---

23. I also collected data in Virgil's *Aeneid*, but because this text has a slightly different behaviour as to the Tense parameter (cf. note 11 above) I leave them out of the present discussion.

(or at least a number of them) occur relatively more often in direct and indirect speech than in the narrative sections. *Ergo* and *enim*, for instance, are found in almost 50% of their occurrences in direct or indirect speech, which is significant considering that the general proportion of direct and indirect speech in narrative texts obviously must be much lower than that. Another interesting observation is that the 'interactional' particles *enim* and *ergo* occur significantly more often in direct and indirect speech than their non-interactional pendants *nam* and *igitur*: 19% for *igitur* against 46% for *ergo*; and 22% for *nam* against 45% for *enim*. This second observation supports the conclusion in Kroon (1995) that *enim* and *nam*, and also *ergo* and *igitur*, have clearly distinct discourse functions, the one involving interactional features, the other not. Note, however, that such a difference in distribution cannot be observed for *autem* versus *vero* and *at*.

Of the remaining instances I registered the tense of the main clause involved, as can be seen in figure 4: perfect, imperfect, pluperfect, historic present, historic infinitive and actual present. In theory, a distinction should have been made also between narrative perfect and authorial perfect, but in practice such a distinction proved to be very hard to make, owing to a lack of objective criteria. The category 'other' contains three categories of instances: (i) the morphologically ambiguous cases of the type *venit*; (ii) instances of ellipsis of the verb (found especially with *vero*); and (iii) cases in which it is hard to determine whether the particle belongs to a main or a subordinate clause (a category which is, again, most relevant for *vero*).

figure 4: correlation between particles and tenses (rounded percentages)

	perf.	imperf.	pluperf.	hist. pr.	hist. inf.	act. pr.	other
at (149)	31%	19%	8%	21%	9%	2%	10%
autem (153)	22%	48%	7%	8%	-	6%	9%
enim (263)	25%	40%	20%	2%	-	9%	4%
ergo (78)	54%	4%	1%	22%	-	1%	18%
igitur (207)	48%	9%	2%	27%	6%	2%	5%
nam (484)	33%	30%	16%	4%	-	9%	8%
vero (115)	24%	12%	1%	14%	20%	3%	26%

4. Conclusions from the statistical data

The diagram in figure 4 is to be read as follows. There are, for instance, 149 usable instances of *at* in the corpus (i.e. instances of *at* in indicative main clauses that do not belong to a direct or indirect speech). In 31% of these instances the main predicate has a perfect tense, in 19% an imperfect, etc. When viewed in isolation (i.e. horizontally) these figures are not very revealing. They would become more interesting, of course, if we also had figures of the absolute frequency of the tenses concerned (preferably in the same narrative corpus and under the same conditions, viz. indicative main clauses with the exclusion of direct and indirect speech), with which the figures in figure 4 could be compared. Such exact data on the absolute frequency of all of the tenses involved are not available. However, a rough indication of the relative frequency of three of the tenses involved (perfect, imperfect and pluperfect) could be deduced from the figures in the diagram below. They are based on an automatic counting of these tenses in a corpus that corresponds to mine to a large degree, but which inevitably does include direct and indirect speech.[24]

figure 5: absolute frequency of perfect, imperfect and pluperfect in a corresponding corpus

tense	absolute frequency
perfect	3918 (63%)
imperfect	1802 (29%)
pluperfect	465 (8%)
total	6185

---

24. The statistics in fig. 5 come from the database of lemmatized and analyzed Latin texts of the *Laboratoire d'Analyse Statistique des Langues Anciennes (LASLA) de l'Université de Liège*. They are based on all indicative main clauses with a perfect, imperfect or pluperfect in Caesar *Gal.*; *Civ.* I; Sallust *Cat.*; *Jug.*; Tacitus *Ann.* XIII-XV; Petronius; and excerpts from Livy (18.000 words). Because of the impossibility of distinguishing, in automatic countings, between the historic present and the actual present, I have not included here the figures for the present. For comparable reasons there are no figures for the historic infinitive. I thank Gerald Purnelle of the *LASLA* for his kind assistance.

From the data in figure 5 it appears that the perfect is more than twice as frequent as the imperfect, and about eight times as frequent as the pluperfect.[25] When comparing these proportions to those of the perfect, imperfect and pluperfect in sentences containing one of the particles studied (see fig. 4) we find a number of interesting differences which indeed seem to suggest the existence of certain correlations between particles and tenses. The most striking observations in this respect are that in *autem* and *enim*-clauses the frequency proportions between perfect and imperfect are more or less reversed, and that in *ergo*- and *igitur*-clauses the use of the perfect (as compared to that of the imperfect and pluperfect) is much more frequent than in general.

More solid conclusions can be drawn, however, when the figures in figure 4 are viewed vertically, that is, when a comparison is made between the proportions of one particle and those of the others. Although there are, of course, no minimal pairs of the type '*igitur* occurs exclusively with the perfect, *nam* with the imperfect', and there are only a few combinations that seem to be really excluded, there appear to be interesting differences between the particles with regard to the proportions in which the various tenses occur. These differences are of such a nature that it seems indeed justified to assume a certain correlation between the two parameters. They indicate, at the same time, that current views on these particles on the one hand, and on narrative tenses on the other, are basically correct. By way of illustration I will mention a few of the implications contained by figure 4.

Much in accordance with my expectations it appears from figure 4 that the combination of *igitur* with the imperfect or pluperfect is not very common. I came across this combination in only 11% of the instances (viz. in 2% and 9%, respectively). This percentage is very low when compared to e.g. *enim* and *nam*, which are combined with an imperfect or pluperfect in 60% and 46%, respectively. The figures in the diagram also appear to corroborate the specific discourse function I assume for *at* in narrative texts (e.g. in comparison with another adversative-like particle as *autem*): it turns out that *at* is relatively often combined with main-line tenses, especially with the historic present and the historic infinitive (note that I did not find any instances of the historic infinitive with *autem*). Also significant are the comparable scores for *at* and *vero* with respect to these two

---

25. Although the inclusion of direct and indirect speech might have raised the figures for the perfect to a larger extent than the figures for the imperfect and pluperfect, it is not to be expected that exclusion of direct and indirect speech would lead to an altogether different picture of the mutual proportions.

tenses, which might be explained on account of the fact that they both occur in contexts with a surprising, counter-expectational content.

About the distribution of tenses with *vero* many interesting things could be said, but I confine myself here to the remark that the study of the distribution of tenses with *vero* provided me with more insight into the linguistic features of prominently presented narrative segments. Such segments appear to be characterized, not only by the use of particular particles (such as *vero*) and tenses (historic present and historic infinitive),[26] but for instance also by the use of 'resumptive' constructions with a focus-signalling function, of the type *cum ... tum vero*. A representative example is (9), which combines the use of the interactional particle *vero* with a recapitulative focus construction (*postquam ..., tum ...*) and the use of a historic present (*invadit*).

(9)   Quod postquam auditum est, tum vero ingens metus nostros invadit. (Sal. *Jug.* 106.6)
        'After hearing this message our soldiers were seized by an extremely great fear.'

Also significant is the observation that *vero*-clauses often lack a (finite) predicate, which might be taken as another feature of an affective or vivid (and hence prominent) presentation. Affectivity (i.e. personal involvement of the narrator, or of a character of the narrated world from whose perspective the events are presented) may also be attained by the use of deictic expressions which refer to immediacy rather than remoteness, as is the case in example (10), in which not only *vero* and the use of the historic present may be taken as indications of an affective mode of presentation, but also the use of *hic* ('here'):

(10)   Interim confecta frumentatione milites nostri clamorem exaudiunt; praecurrunt equites; quanto res sit in periculo cognoscunt. Hic vero nulla munitio est quae perterritos recipiat: ... (Caes. *Gal.* 6.39.1-2)

---

26. When compared to e.g. the percentages for *at*, *ergo* and *igitur*, the combination of *vero* with the historic present might seem to be not particularly frequent. However, the relatively low percentage is due to the frequent occurrence of the historic infinitive with *vero*, and to the fact that 26% of the *vero*-instances belong to the category 'other' (which e.g. includes ellipsis of the verb). Note that the categories 'historic present', 'historic infinitive' and 'other' together constitute about 60% of all *vero*-instances.

'Meanwhile, having finished corn-gathering, our troops heard the shouting; the cavalry sped forward, and learnt the great danger of the moment. But here was no entrenchment to receive the scared soldiers: ...'

Departing, not from the particles, but from the tenses in figure 4, especially the distribution of the historic infinitive may attract our attention. It appears to be frequent to any extent with some of the particles only, viz. with *at* (14 instances), *igitur* (13 instances) and especially *vero* (23 instances out of a total of 115 instances of *vero*). What these particles have in common is, in any case, that they are typical main-line markers, with in the case of *at* and *vero* a clear preference for narrative prominence. Especially the high degree of compatibility of *vero* with the historic infinitive might be of use in attempts to get more insight into the discourse function of the historic infinitive.

Besides figures and proportions that appear to confirm my hypotheses, figure 4 also contains a few results that I did *not* expect, such as the relatively high percentage of the imperfect with *autem*. Closer inspection of the data reveals, however, that in historical prose (which makes up the bulk of my corpus) *autem* is predominantly used for marking a rather specific type of thematic shifts, viz. shifts from a major discourse topic to a secondary discourse topic, after which 'digression' the interrupted major thematic chain is resumed.[27] Such segments are clear instances of what I call 'subsidiary information'. The frequent use of the imperfect with *autem* is therefore quite explainable. Example (11) serves as an illustration:

(11)   Eo cum venisset (sc. Caesar), animum advertit ad alteram fluminis ripam magnas esse copias hostium instructas. Ripa *autem* erat acutis sudibus praefixis munita ... His rebus cognitis ... Caesar praemisso equitatu confestim legiones subsequi iussit. (Caes. *Gal.* 5.18.2-4)
'When he (sc. Caesar) was come thither he remarked that on the other bank of the river a great force of the enemy was drawn up. The bank *autem* was fortified with a fringe of sharp projecting stakes ... When he had learned these details ... Caesar sent the cavalry in advance and ordered the legions to follow up instantly.'

27. See Kroon (1995: 267-269).

What is most intriguing in figure 4, however, is the distribution of tenses with *nam*, which will be the subject of a more detailed discussion in the following section.

5. The distribution of tenses with *nam*

Departing from the characteristic and, as far as I know, undisputed discourse function of *nam* (viz. the marking of marginal text segments which support more central text segments), one might expect this particle to be combined relatively often with the imperfect and pluperfect. An example of this expected pattern is (12), in which *nam* is combined with the imperfect *prohibebat*:

(12)   Romani ex inproviso pulveris vim magnam animadvortunt; *nam* prospectum ager arbustis consitus *prohibebat*. (Sal. *Jug.* 53.1)
'Suddenly the Romans noticed an enormous dust cloud; for the undergrowth overgrowing the terrain obstructed their view.'

However, from figure 4 it appears that there is no significant predominance of the imperfect with *nam*. On the contrary, in only 30% of the instances in our corpus *nam* occurs with an imperfect, while for *enim* this is 40% and for *autem* even 48%. Moreover, the instances of *nam* with a perfect outnumber those with an imperfect.[28] The question to be answered is, of course, whether these figures prove that something is wrong, either with our definition of the discourse function of *nam*, or with current opinions about the function of the Latin imperfect. A closer study of the perfect-cases involved fortunately reassures us on this point, but it also warns us against counting instances, in a research like this, in a too mechanic way.

First of all, when we look at the figures of the individual authors in the corpus, it turns out that in Sallust the situation is as expected: besides 32 instances of the imperfect with *nam*, we find only 4 instances of the perfect, three of which clearly belong, moreover, to the *expositio* and not to the *narratio*. In Livy, however, the situation is inverse. Here, we find 56 imperfect-cases against 111 instances of the perfect. And in the other authors of the corpus the proportion of imperfect-cases and perfect-cases is more or less fifty-fifty.

---

28. Comparable figures can be found in Bolkestein (1991: 432), on the basis of a different corpus.

A possible explanation for the high number of perfective *nam*-instances in Livy might be, of course, that the majority belong to the exposition layer of the text and thus that we are dealing in fact with the authorial use of the perfect. This, however, is not the case. Although *nam* is not excluded with the authorial perfect, as is demonstrated by example (1), by far the most instances of *nam* with a perfect tense appear to belong to the narration proper, and to be part of a typically Livian narrative technique. This technique is illustrated by example (13).

(1)   Augur in locum eius inauguratus Q. Fabius Maximus filius; in eiusdem locum pontifex — *nam* duo sacerdotia *habuit* — Ser. Sulpicius Galba. (Liv. 30.26.10)
        'In his place as augur his son Quintus Fabius Maximus was installed; likewise in his place as pontifex — for he held two priesthoods — Servius Sulpicius Galba.'

(13)   Haud inultum interfecere; *nam* circa repugnantem aliquot insidiatores *cecidere* (...) (Liv. 3.43.4)
        'He died not unavenged. For he laid about him, and several of the assassins fell (...)'

This technique involves the use of an established pattern, consisting of a preview of a narrative episode coming up, and the actual episode itself which is introduced by *nam*. The preview (in ex. 13 the clause *haud inultum interfecere*) is usually stated in very general, non-specific terms and often contains an element of authorial evaluation (like *haud inultum* in ex. 13). On account of the fact that these preview-sentences do not belong themselves to the stepwise development of the narrative, but rather have an evaluating or procedural function, we might assign them to the exposition layer of the text, the actual *narratio* starting with the *nam*-clause. On the one hand this narrative can be considered a support (in the form of a narrative episode) of the preceding clause that belongs to the exposition-layer. This support-function explains the use of *nam*. On the other hand the state of affairs described in the *nam*-clause functions also as the first essential step in the now developing narrative, which explains the use of the perfect tense. In other words, the function of the *nam*-clause can be described in two different ways, each correponding to a different layer of the text. The particle *nam* is to be described and explained by referring to the exposition layer, the use of the perfect by referring to the narration-layer.[29] Within this view it is not surprising that, in the *nam*-clause of the pattern, we may also come across the historic present instead of the perfect, as can be seen in (14).[30]

(14)   Memorandum deinde edidere facinus; *nam* Staium Minatium ducem adeuntem ordines hortantemque *invadunt*; (...) (Liv. 10.20.13)
'They presently performed a remarkable exploit; for as Staius Minatius, the Samnite general, was riding along the ranks and encouraging them, they made a rush at him; (...)'

This particular narrative technique is not used by Sallust, which explains why in this author we find the hypothesized high degree of compatibility of *nam* with the imperfect. The other authors in the corpus do use the technique, but more sparingly than Livy. Example (15) is taken from Caesar, (16) from Tacitus. In (15) the segment introduced by *nam* more or less functions as an explanation, in the form of a *narratio*, of the evaluating expression *magno usui*. The perfect forms *constituerunt* and *rettulerunt* are two successive events within this *narratio*. Example (16) is comparable: *vitavit* counts as a preannouncement, in very general, unspecific terms, of the specific events to be described in the *narratio* starting in the next clause.

(15)   Quae res magno usui nostris fuit. *Nam* ... barbari *constiterunt* ac paulum modo pedem *rettulerunt*. (...) (Caes. *Gal.* 4.25.2)
'This moment proved of great service to our troops; for the natives ... came to a halt, and retired, but only for a little space. (...)'

(16)   Unde in regionem Tauraunitium transgressus improvisum periculum vitavit (sc. Corbulo). *Nam* haud procul tentorio eius non ignobilis barbarus cum

---

29. The conclusion should therefore be that in instances like (13) there is in fact no correlation between the particle and the tense used.
30. The occurrence of the historic present in this example proves, in my opinion, that *cecidere* in example (13) is a narrative and not an authorial perfect. The 'authorial' perfects in the introductory sentences of (13) and (14), on the other hand, are not likely to have a present tense alternative. Sporadically, we also find the pattern with an imperfect tense in the *nam* clause, e.g. Liv. 3.26.3 and 30.13.9. The use of the imperfect in these instances can however be explained on independent grounds: in 3.26.3 the imperfect is used in a preparatory part of the narrative; in 30.13.9 the imperfect is used for a 'pictorial presentation' of an event on the main story-line (usage b in the left-hand row of figure 1).

telo repertus ordinem insidiarum seque auctorem et socios per tormenta *edidit*, ... (Tac. *Ann*. 14.24.3)

'Hence he (sc. Corbulus) crossed into the Tauronite district, where he escaped an unexpected danger. A barbarian of some note, who had been found with a weapon not far from Corbulo's tent, disclosed under torture the whole sequence of the plot, his own responsibility for it, and his accomplices, ...'

As a corollary we can say that, for a proper analysis of the use of the tenses in cases like (12) - (16), it is necessary to distinguish between support on the exposition-layer (as is the case in 13 - 16), and support on the narration-layer (as in 12). In contrast to (12), in (13) - (16) the Particle parameter and the Tense parameter operate at different layers of the text. They are therefore not good examples for illustrating the correlation between the two parameters.

This detailed study of the distribution of narrative tenses with *nam* demonstrates, thus, that, at least from a linguistic viewpoint, it is useful to distinguish various layers in a narrative text, for instance a narration-layer and an exposition-layer, as suggested in figure 1: narrative texts involve a constant alternation of *narratio* and *expositio* and this insight is essential for explaining certain less expected combinations of particles and tenses.

6. Conclusions

Within the limited scope of this article I have made an attempt to shed more light, from a linguistic point of view, on the complex phenomenon of narrative text structure. The correlation research presented here not only shows that current views on the discourse functions of Latin tenses and particles are basically correct, but also serves as an illustration of one possible way to get more grip on such contentious and ill-defined notions as *foreground* and *background*, and *narratio* and *expositio*. More research, involving more parameters, is of course required, in which special attention should be given to determining objective criteria for the distinction between narration and exposition (or comparable notions). The main concern of my paper has been, however, to show how in a study dealing with narrative structure linguistic and more literary approaches may fruitfully supplement each other.

Bibliography

Benveniste, E.
  1966 *Problèmes de linguistique générale, I.* Paris: Gallimard
Bolkestein, A.M.
  1991 Causally related predications and the choice between parataxis and hypotaxis in Latin. In: R. Coleman (ed.) *New Studies in Latin Linguistics.* Amsterdam: Benjamins, p. 427-451
Chausserie-Laprée, J.R.
  1969 *L'expression narrative chez les historiens latins.* Paris: De Boccard
Fleischmann, S.
  1990 *Tense and Narrativity. From medieval Performance to modern Fiction.* London: Routledge
Kroon, C.H.M.
  1995 *Discourse Particles in Latin: A Study of* nam, enim, autem, vero *and* at. Amsterdam: Gieben
Kroon, C.H.M. & P.J. Rose
  1996 *Atrociter corruptus?* The use of 'narrative' tenses in Ammianus Marcellinus' *Res Gestae.* In: R. Risselada *et al.* (eds.) *On Latin. Linguistic and literary Studies in Honour of Harm Pinkster.* Amsterdam: Gieben, p. 71-89
Mellet, S.
  1984 Présent de narration et parfait dans le conte de Psyché. *Revue des Études Latines* 63, 148-160
Pinkster, H.
  1983 Tempus, Aspect and Aktionsart in Latin (Recent trends 1961-1981). *Aufstieg und Niedergang der römischen Welt* 29:1, 270-320
  1990 *Latin Syntax and Semantics.* London: Routledge.
Quinn, K.
  1968 *Virgil's Aeneid. A critical Description.* London: Routledge
Rosén, H.
  1980 "Exposition und Mitteilung". The imperfect as a thematic tense-form in the Letters of Pliny. In: H. Rosén & H.B. Rosén, *On Moods and Tenses of the Latin Verb.* Munich: Fink, p. 27-48
  1995 The Latin *infinitivus historicus* revisited. *Mnemosyne* 48, 536-564
Serbat, G.
  1988 Le prétendu "présent de l'indicatif": une forme non-déictique du verbe. *l'Information Grammaticale* 38, 32-36
Stouthart, H.
  n.d. Het imperfectum bij Vergilius. Onderzoek naar het gedrag van imperfecta in boek 2 en 6 van de *Aeneis.* Ms. Classics Dept., Vrije Universiteit Amsterdam
Wehr, B.
  1984 *Diskursstrategien im Romanischen.* Tübingen: Narr
Weinrich, H.
  1964 *Tempus. Besprochene und erzählte Welt.* Stuttgart: Kohlhammer

Is the Latin present tense the unmarked, neutral tense in the system?

Harm Pinkster

The present tense in Latin can be used for events that do not coincide with but either precede or follow the actual communicative situation in which the tense is used. In several recent studies this fact has been explained by assuming a neutral or non-temporal value for the present tense. This paper presents a detailed examination of the conditions under which the present tense is actually used, especially in past narratives in orations of Cicero. This examination shows that the present tense cannot be regarded as simply replacing other (past and future) tenses nor as simply replaceable by other tenses. It has its own semantic value in the overall tense system.

0. Introduction

In the Latin verbal system the present tense is the tense that a speaker or writer used to present events or situations as contemporaneous with the communicative setting in which he produced his utterance. A trivial example of this use is (1):

(1) aetatem meam *scis? # scio* esse grandem, item ut pecuniam. #
     certe edepol equidem te civem sine mala omni malitia
     semper sum arbitratus et nunc *arbitror. #* aurum huic *olet.*
     quid nunc me *vis? #* quoniam tu me et ego te qualis sis *scio ...*
     filiam tuam mi uxorem *posco.* (Pl. *Aul.* 214-219)
     'You know my age? # Getting on, getting on, I know that, financially too.
     # Now Euclio, I've always considered you a citizen of the true, trusty type,
     by Jove, I certainly have, and I do still. # He's got a whiff of my gold. Well,
     what do you want? # Now that we appreciate each other, I'm going to ask
     you ... to give me your daughter in marriage.'

The decision to present something as contemporaneous with the speech situation or not is to some extent free and up to the speaker (writer).[1] A good example of the use of a non-present tense to refer to something which is actually taking place

---

1. A number of 'atypical' uses of tenses are discussed by Klein (1994: 133-141).

in the speech situation is the so-called epistolary imperfect as in (2) (see Recanati 1995) and the so-called polite use of the imperfect as in (3) (see Pinkster 1990: 229):

(2)   Nihil *habebam* quod scriberem. (Cic. *Att.* 9.10.1)
       'I have nothing to write.'

(3)   sed si domi est, Demaenetum *volebam*. (Pl. *As.* 452)
       'But I wished to see Demaenetus, if he is at home.'

In (2) Cicero reports he has nothing to write about while writing and in (3) Demaenetus is wanted at that very moment. Still, for reasons well discussed in the literature, the speaker (writer) locates the events outside the communicative setting and chooses the imperfect tense. In a similar way the present tense is used in situations in which from a purely chronometric point of view a future or past tense might be possible or even more appropriate. In (4), for example, the meal will take place later, in the evening of that day, and in (5) the speaker has heard the news before uttering *audio*.

(4)   et is hodie apud me *cenat* et frater meus; (Pl. *St.* 415)
       'And now he's to dine with me today, he and my brother too;'

(5)   ... id ego feci et fateor. # quid ego ex te *audio*? (Pl. *Aul.* 734)
       '... I'm to blame, and I confess it, sir. # Hey? What's that?

From Antiquity onwards philosophers and linguists have found difficulty in explaining the use of the present tense in utterances referring to events that are, strictly speaking, situated outside the communicative setting of the Speaker and Addressee or in utterances that refer, more narrowly, to events situated before or after the speech situation. Philosophers have time and again denied that there is such a thing as a 'now' in the ongoing movement of time.[2] In view of the use of the present in such situations many linguists have objected to defining the value of the present tense as 'presents the state of affairs as simultaneous with the communicative setting (or: the speech situation)'.

     Several latinists working in a more or less strictly defined structural framework (Serbat in several publications, most recently 1988; Mellet 1985; Mellet *et al.* 1994: 21-52; Moralejo 1988; Touratier 1994: 94-101; 1996) regard the present tense as the 'unmarked', 'neutral', 'zero' or 'atemporal' tense in the overall tense

---

2. For a historical survey of the debate see Serbat (1976) and Mellet *et al.* (1994).

system, which explains why it can be used instead of other tenses.[3] Similar views were held by diachronically working linguists in the beginning of this century who explained the historical present as a variety of the 'achronistic' or 'timeless' value of the present tense, which can be found from Indo-European onwards (a summary in Bennett 1910:10-17). Serbat (1976) and Mellet (1985) have also drawn attention to the fact that most present tense forms can be described as morphologically unmarked (*ama-t* : *ama-ba-t* and *ama-bi-t*).[4]

The use of the present as a narrative tense to refer to past events and situations (the so-called historical present) is a special point in case. In structural approaches to the tense system this use of the present is taken as further evidence for the unmarked value of the present. Quantitative observations are also taken as support for this approach: the present is so overwhelmingly frequent that it is best taken as a basic narrative tense *tout court*.

The same quantitative observations are also the starting point for Von Albrecht's article (1970) on the use of the tenses in Virgil. According to Von Albrecht the present and the perfect are exchangeable as far as their semantic value is concerned (1970: 224) and literary artists, Virgil in particular, use the choice between them to structure the narrative and to highlight certain episodes by using the perfect tense.[5] In fact, Mellet's (1985) article, while assuming a non-temporal function for the present tense, discusses the function of the perfect much along the same lines.

In traditional attempts to explain the historical present psychological (or stylistic, in the terminology of Szantyr, p. 307) considerations have been brought forward. In this approach the speaker/author *presents* the event as 'present' (or: 'actual') although, using a stopwatch or some other time measuring device, the event is not really 'present' or 'actual'. Quintilian's description of the use of the present in past narratives as an instance of metaphor (*Inst.* 9.2.41-43, 9.3.11) is the earliest along these lines (cf. Weinrich 1964: ch. 5). In my (1983) paper I have also described the use of the historical present basically along these lines, *viz.* as a way of presenting past events as if it were an eyewitness account.

I will once more try to demonstrate that the present tense is excluded in certain contexts and situations and that, conversely, when the present is used,

---

3. Moralejo makes a distinction between 'unmarked' and 'negative' use of the present tense for the historical and future use on the one hand and the actual present on the other. Objections in Touratier (1994). Recent discussions of a general character can be found in Fleischman (1990, especially ch. 2) and Recanati (1995).
4. Reservations on the usefulness of this type of consideration can be found in Moralejo (1988:30).
5. Von Albrecht's article, inspiring as it is, has had some influence on commentators, especially his idea that the present and perfect are in principle exchangeable. See, for example, Töchterle (1994) *ad* Sen. *Oed.* 48, 133ff. I have formulated my criticism of this article in Pinkster (1983: 309-310).

outside its proper domain so to speak, it cannot always be replaced by a future or past form either. I will also try to show that, at least in Cicero, the use of the historical present correlates with other linguistic phenomena, which makes it impossible to regard the historical present as used 'instead of' the regular past tenses. This range of uses can best be explained on the basis of its own semantic value ('contemporaneity with the speech situation') and of the semantic values of the other tenses that are required in those contexts and situations.[6]

1. The present tense used to refer to future events

The best description of the use of the present for states of affairs that are, strictly speaking, situated after the speech situation is still Sjögren (1906). From this study it has become clear that there are specific situations in which the future cannot be replaced by the present and, conversely, also specific uses of the present which cannot be replaced by the future. Examples of both types are (6)-(8) and (9)-(13), respectively:

(6)   Hoc quidem hercle, quoquo *ibo*, mecum *erit*, mecum *feram*,
        neque isti id in tantis periclis umquam *committam* ut siet. (Pl. *Aul.* 449-450)
        'By heaven, wherever I go this goes too: I won't leave it there to run such risks never.'

(7)   multa scio faciunda verba. *ibo* intro. sed apertast foris. (Pl. *St.* 87)
        'It'll take a lot of talking, that's sure. Well. I'll go in. But the door's open.'

(8)   *accedam* propius. (Pl. *Cas.* 577)
        'I'll step up to her.'

Sjögren has numerous examples to show that in asides such as (6)-(8), but also in other types of context the future is required.

(9)   mane:
        iam *redeo* ad te. # at maturate propera, nam propero: vides
        iam diem multum esse. # video: hunc advocare etiam volo;

---

6. My own ideas on the tense system as a whole and the semantic values of the individual tenses can be found in Pinkster (1983) and the chapter on tense in Pinkster (1990). I had the pleasure to work on this article with the 1995 class in Latin Linguistics. I am grateful for the cooperation with Xander van Eckeren, Astrid Landa, Marijke Ottink, Irene von Oven, Wim Remmelink, Mira Tax, and Petra Wisse. I have especially used data investigated by Irene and Wim.

mane modo istic, iam revortar ad te. (Pl. *Ps.* 1156-1159)
'Wait! I'll soon be back. # But hurry fast, for I am in a hurry: you see how late it is already. # I see. I only want a little advice from him. Just you wait there: I'll soon rejoin you.'

(10) salve, mi pater. # et vos ambae. ilico agite adsidite. #
osculum. # sat est osculi mihi vostri. # qui, amabo, pater? #
quia ita meae animae salsura evenit. # adside hic, pater. #
non *sedeo* isti, vos sedete; ego sedero in subsellio. #
mane, pulvinum— # bene procuras. mihi satis sic fultumst. sede. #
sine, pater. (Pl. *St.* 90-95)
'Good morning, father dear! # Same to you both. That'll do, that'll do, sit down! # Just a kiss. # I've had enough of your kissing. # Oh, father dear, how can you say that? # Because it already has made my breath briny. # Sit down here, father. # Not I, you two sit there. I'll sit on this bench myself. # Wait, a cushion! # You do take good care of me. There, there, that's plenty of propping. Sit down. # Just one more, father.'

(11) et is hodie apud me *cenat* et frater meus; (Pl. *St.* 415)
'And now he's to dine with me today, he and my brother too;'

(12) scin quid ego te volebam? # dic. # *cras* est mihi
iudicium. # quid tum? # ut diligenter nunties ... (Ter. *Eun.* 338)
'Do you know what I wanted to say to you? # No. # I have an action on tomorrow. # Yes, and? # Mind you tell ...'

(13)   feriam fores.
aperite hoc. heus, ecquis hic est? ecquis hoc *aperit* ostium? (Pl. *Am.*
1019-1020)
'I'll knock. Open up here! Hey! Is anyone in? Open, somebody!'

Example (9) is an illustration of the use of the present tense referring to an event that is going to take place in the near future in the communicative setting. Expressions of the type 'I'll be back in a second' are normally in the present tense. The future form *revortar* in line 1159 of this example seems to be an exception. It has been noted by Sjögren (1906: 8) that the verb *reverti* has always future tense in Plautus, as in this example, suggesting that this is a lexical feature of *reverti*. However, *reverti* is not used in the same type of context as *redire* and this explains the difference in use of the tenses.[7] In (10) we have an example of the use of the present in negative reactions to commands or invitations. In (11) we see an example of a fixed date for some social event for later on the day. In (12) we see one of the rare combinations of *cras* with a present tense form, for something that is fixed in the calendar.[8] (13), finally, expresses Amphitruo's amazement and impatience when he finds his door closed. As Sjögren has shown, in all these circumstances the present is required or at least preferred.

The examples show that, measuring by the stopwatch, there are situations in which the present is used to refer to events 'after now'. Even so there seem to be different rules governing the use of the future and that of the present, and there is no reason to call one or the other unmarked or neutral. Given the fact that the present is not really used 'instead of' the future, it is also questionable whether there is a need for characterising the use of the present in these cases as 'more decisive', or 'more urgent', as some linguists and philologists do.[9]

2. The present tense used to refer to general events

Another use of the present tense is its use in statements about general truths, as in (14), an example discussed by Serbat (1976) and Touratier (1994):

(14)   audentes fortuna *iuvat*. (Verg. *A*. 10.284)
       'Fortune aids the daring.'

Although it is true that this statement is meant to be relevant in a general way to all periods of mankind, it is nonetheless presented as a general truth that is relevant in the communicative setting. This becomes clear if we replace the present tense form by either a future or a past tense form. The statement will remain a general statement, but, if stated in the future or past form, not be considered relevant to

---

7. The future form *revortar* is either used for someone entering the scene or when there is some doubt about how much time it will take for someone to return.
8. The normal tense is the future. Indicative present tense forms are rare among the instances mentioned in *TLL*, s.v. 1099.29ff. Another example, where the future is impossible, is Cic. *Fam.* 16.23.2 *cras expecto Leptam* ('tomorrow I am expecting Lepta'). A different analysis is possible for the only indicative instance in Plautus:
                                   ei rei dies
       haec praestituta est, proxuma Dionysia. #
       cras ea quidem *sunt*: prope adest exitium mihi, ... (Pl. *Ps*. 58-60)
       'The day fixed upon for all this is the next Dionysia. # Hm! That's tomorrow: my doom is close at hand, ...'
9. So, for example, Szantyr (p. 308).

the actual communicative setting. Therefore, I would not call the use of the present tense in such statements unmotivated or unmarked.

3. The present tense used to refer to past events in non-narrative texts

Before passing to the much debated issue of the historical present I will present a few examples in which the present refers to events, which 'on the stopwatch', are past:

(15)   ... id ego feci et fateor. # quid ego ex te *audio*? (Pl. *Aul.* 734)
       '... I'm to blame, and I confess it, sir. # Hey? What's that?'

(16)   verum quod tu *dicis*, mea uxor, non te mi irasci decet. (Pl. *Am.* 522)
       'But as to what you say, precious, you oughtn't to be cross with me.'

(17)   Calchantem augurem *scribit* Homerus longe optumum ... fuisse ... (Cic. *Div.*
       1.87)
       'For example, Homer writes that Calchas was by far the best augur ...'

In (15) *audio* refers to the immediately preceding words. In (16) Alcumena's words are eight lines back, after an interruption of Alcumena's and Jupiter's conversation by Mercurius. Examples like these are quite common (Kühner-Stegmann: I, 117-118). In the Plautine cases (Lodge 1924: 189) of surprised or indignant questions as in (15), where the content of the information is the focal element, the present seems to be required. The perfect is found when the fact of hearing or the location in time is focal. Something similar seems to be the case in Cicero's use of *audio* vs *audivi* in the Verrine orations.[10] Back reference to the words of a partner in a dialogue as in (16) and in expressions like *ut dicis* (Lodge 1924: 383) in the present tense is normal. In the only *ut dixisti* example in Plautus[11] the focal element is the fact that the partner has promised to do something earlier in the comedy (in line 1157). (17) is an instance of the so-called citative use of the present, also a quite common phenomenon. Wisse (1996) demonstrates that pragmatic differences of the type just mentioned correlate with the use of the present and perfect in Cicero's use of *dicere*.

10. Mathieu de Bakker (ass. report 1996).
11. ... tuam, ut *dixisti*, mihi desponde filiam. (Pl. *Poen.* 1357) '... promise me your daughter as you said.'

In (18) below, the old man Simo has left the house and, alone on the scene, is talking to himself (or the audience). *Iubet* definitely refers to a suggestion of his wife in the preceding scene. However, her order is still relevant for the present moment, as the adverb *nunc* shows. She still wants Simo to go to bed. In (19) *venis* refers to the arrival of Pamphilippus, which actually has taken place some time ago. The Loeb translation runs: 'How long since you got into port?'.[12] It is explained, as the earlier example, as a past event having current relevance by Kühner-Stegmann (I, p. 117) and by Petersmann (1973) *a.l.*, but it is surely the most problematic one among the 'present perfect' instances given in Bennett (1910: 17-18). My explanation is that Epignomus is not asking *when* his brother arrived, but expresses his amazement at the fact that he is arriving so late. I therefore prefer an exclamation mark instead of a question mark.

(18)   prandium uxor mihi perbonum dedit,
        nunc dormitum *iubet* me ire: minime. (Pl. *Mos.* 692-693)
        'That was a luscious lunch my wife gave me! And now she tells me to go and take a nap! Not a bit of it!'

(19)   sed eccum fratrem Pamphilippum, incedit cum socero suo. #
        quid agitur, Epignome? # quid tu? quam dudum in portum *venis!* #
        huc longissume postilla[13] (Pl. *St.* 527-529)
        But there's my brother Pamphilippus strolling along with his father-in-law. #'How goes it, Epignomus? # And with you? How late that you got into port! # Here a long time thereafter.'

The examples of the present in utterances referring to the past discussed so far are the counterpart of the *praesens pro futuro* instances discussed in section 1. There are distributional differences between the present when used to refer to past events and the perfect which can best be explained on the basis of their semantic values.

---

12. For an instance with a perfect tense see Pl. *As.* 449 *quam dudum tu advenisti?* ('How long have you been here?') For *quam dudum* with a present tense see Pl. *St.* 310 *vide quam dudum hic asto et pulto.* ('See how long I have to stand here and knock.'). Note that in the latter example we find the indicative mood, which suggests that it is an exclamation (cf. Bolkestein 1995b).
13. Petersmann (1973) reads *Hau* instead of *huc*, as others did before him. The whole passage is difficult to interpret. See Petersmann (1973) *a.l.*

4. The use of the present tense in past narratives

I will now turn to the historical present, which has provoked energetic discussions among latinists until quite recently. I will summarize well-known observations made on the comedies of Plautus and Terence and then proceed to two narrative pieces in orations of Cicero.

In Plautus and Terence, whenever one of the characters describes past events in the present tense, ambiguity in the speech situation between 'actual' and 'historical' present is avoided by various signals such as introductory or concluding perfect tenses and/or situating adverbs and connectors, such as *ibi* and *atque ... illi* in the following examples (Heinze 1924; Hofmann 1950: 173). Such expressions facilitate the interpretation of the change from 'here and now' to 'there and then'.

(20) postquam illam sunt conspicatae, quam tuo' gnatus deperit:
      "quam facile et quam fortunate evenit illi, opsecro,
      mulieri quam liberare volt amator!" "quisnam is est?"
      inquit altera illi. *ibi* illa *nominat* Stratippoclem. (Pl. *Epid.* 242-245)
      'After they spied that girl your son is daft over: "Mercy me," says she, "the easy, lucky way things do come to that girl, with her lover wanting to set her free!" "Who on earth is he?" says the other. Then the first one names him, Stratippocles, the son of Periphanes.'

(21) forte fortuna per impluvium huc despexi in proxumum:
      atque ego *illi aspicio* osculantem Philocomasium cum altero
      nescioquo adulescente. (Pl. *Mil.* 287-289)
      'I just happened to happen to look down through the skylight into the house next door here, and there I spied Philocomasium and some other young fellow kissing each other.'

The sentences with a historical present are embedded in the discourse structure and occur in that part of the narrative which Labov (1972: 354-396) labels 'complicating action' (cf. Myhill 1992: 62 ff., Chafe 1994: 207-210). The effect of this is that particularly salient or dramatic events are highlighted in the form of some sort of eyewitness account. This use of the present is no problem for those linguists who, like myself, describe the semantic value of the present tense roughly as 'presenting the event as simultaneous with the speech situation'.

Another type of text where it is essential to mark the transition to the historical present is the *narratio* in Cicero's orations. Just as in the interactive situation on the stage in the Plautine examples, Cicero has to avoid misunderstan-

dings on the part of his audience, the jury.[14] An illustration is the narratio in his
pro Milone (24-29), in which he tells the story of Clodius' and Milo's preparations,
encounter and fight, ending in Clodius' death. The narratio is clearly introduced
as such in the following way:

(22)   Quod quo facilius argumentis perspicere possitis, rem gestam vobis dum
       breviter expono, quaeso, diligenter attendite. (Cic. *Mil.* 23)
       'And in order that in the light of proofs you may get a clearer view of this
       question, please give me your careful attention while I lay before you a short
       narrative of the occurence.'

The section with Clodius' preparations takes about one half of the narratio and is
set in preterite tenses throughout. In § 27 Cicero takes his time in describing
Clodius' departure (*profectus est, profectus est*). Then, in § 28, he turns to his client
Milo, initially continuing with perfect tense forms:

(23)   Milo autem cum in senatu fuisset eo die, quoad senatus est dimissus, domum
       vēnit, calceos et vestimenta mutavit, paulisper, dum se uxor, ut fit, comparat,
       commoratus est, dein profectus id temporis cum iam Clodius, si quidem eo
       die Romam venturus erat, redire potuisset. Obviam *fit* ei Clodius, expeditus,
       ..., cum hic insidiator ... veheretur in raeda ... *Fit* obviam Clodio ante
       fundum eius ... *Statim* complures cum telis in hunc *faciunt* de loco superiore
       impetum; adversi raedarium *occidunt*. Cum ... desiluisset ... caedere *incipiunt*
       eius servos qui post erant; ex quibus qui animo fideli in dominum et
       praesenti fuerunt, partim occisi sunt, partim ... fecerunt id servi Milonis...
       (30) Haec, sicuti exposui, ita gesta sunt, iudices. (Cic. *Mil.* 28-30)
       'Milo, on the other hand, after having been in the Senate that day until its
       dismissal, went home, changed his shoes and his raiment, waited for a short
       time while his wife made such preparations as ladies must make, and finally
       started out so late that Clodius might have already returned to Rome, had
       he ever intended to do so. He was met by Clodius, unencumbered ... while
       our supposed conspirator ... was driving ... in a coach ... He meets Clodius
       in front of his manor ... An attack is immediately made upon my client by
       several armed men posted on higher ground; others stand in the way of the
       coach and kill the coachman; but when Milo ... leapt from the vehicle and
       defended himself with energy, Clodius' party ... began to cut down the slaves

14. Fleischman (1990: 90) rightly distinguishes two types of narrative, that which is 'designed as
absent-author communication (most varieties of written narrative) and narrative designed for
interactive oral performance'.

who were following. Such of these as showed presence of mind and loyalty towards their master were either slain, or Milo's slaves ... did, what ... (30) My narrative, gentlemen, is in exact correspondence with the facts.'

At the critical moment of the confrontation between Milo and Clodius Cicero shifts from the perfect to the present tense, but only so in the main clauses. The *ut fit* expression in the series of perfects cannot cause ambiguity, since it can only be interpreted as a statement of Cicero outside the story line proper. Interesting is the relative clause *qui animo fideli ... fuerunt* with a perfect form (and not the imperfect *erant*), which is a statement of Cicero outside the storyline expressing his subjective, moral judgement about the behaviour of these slaves instead of a description of their personal qualities. The perfects *occisi sunt ... fecerunt* conclude the narratio, the end of which is explicitly indicated by Cicero. There are two extra signals for the audience to mark the shift to a more dramatic narrative mode, *viz.* the placement of the verb phrases *obviam fit* and *fit obviam* in sentence initial position and the sentence initial position of *statim*. Notice that in this narratio the present tense forms are in the minority and that they occur in a cluster.

Another beautiful narrative piece can be found in the last of the Verrine orations, in which Cicero describes the disaster of the Roman fleet (5.86-110) in Sicily.[15] The episode differs in several respects from the narratio in the *pro Milone*. In the first place, it is much longer and much more detailed. Apart from evaluative comments, rhetorical questions, exclamations and parts of the narrative in direct speech, Cicero at certain points in the narrative provides his audience with geographical and historical background information for their better understanding. An example of a succession of a historical present and actual, geographical information is the following:

(24)   (background information in imperfect tense forms about the commander Cleomenes) *Ecce autem repente* ebrio Cleomene, esurientibus ceteris *nuntiatur* piratarum esse naves in portu Odysseae; *nam* ita is locus *nominatur;* nostra autem classis erat in portu Pachyni. (Cic. *Ver.* 5.87)
       'And now, while Cleomenes was drunk and his men starving, the news suddenly arrived that there were pirate ships in the harbour of the place known as Odyssea, our fleet being in the harbour of Pachynus.'

In this passage the historical present is preceded by three signals *ecce, autem,* and *repente* drawing attention to the shift, among which *autem,* which marks the 'transition to a new stage or step in the narrative' (Kroon 1995: 266, and this vol.

---

15. See already Schlicher (1931: 50).

p. 45-46; see also Chausserie-Laprée 1969, especially p. 547, n. 2). The geographical
background information speaks for itself both because of the meaning of *ita* ...
nominatur, but also because of the presence of *nam*. The return to the storyline is
clear from the imperfect tense *erat*.[16]

There is another interesting difference between the historical presents and the
actual presents in this narratio. Whereas the historical presents often occupy the
first position of their sentence or clause, this is exceptional for actual presents, as
can be seen in table 1:

	Total number	In first position[17]
actual present	13	1
historical present	56	31
perfect	29	5
imperfect	41	10

table 1: position in the sentence or main clause of tense forms in Cic. *Ver.* 5.86-110

16. Since Cicero switches often from his own position to the past and back, the interpretation of
present forms may become difficult, at least for some time. This is illustrated by:
> Iste in tabulas refert, obsignat signis amicorum ... ut ... hac videlicet testificatione
> uteretur. Derisum esse credo hominem amentem a suis consiliariis et admonitum
> hasce ei tabulas nihil profuturas ... Iam iste erat hac stultitia multis in rebus usus ut
> publice quoque quae vellet in litteris civitatum tolli et referri iuberet; quae omnia
> nunc *intellegit* sibi nihil prodesse, posteaquam certis litteris, testibus auctoritatibusque
> convincitur. Ubi hoc *videt*, illorum confessionem, testificationem suam, tabellas sibi
> nullo adiumento futuras, *init* consilium ... (Cic. *Ver.* 5.102-103)
> '... which Verres caused to be written down and sealed with his friend's seals, with
> the intention... we may assume, of using this testimony ... as a defence against the
> charge we are considering. I take it that the fool's own councillors laughed at him,
> and pointed out to him that this written record would do him no service ... It was
> by no means the first time that he had employed this stupid device, even ordering
> the official deletion or insertion of passages in various town records to suit his
> wishes; all of which, he is now aware, is doing his cause no good, since there is
> definite authority of written and spoken evidence to prove his guilt. When he saw
> that the captain's statements and his own written records would avail him nothing,
> he embarked on a plan ...'

The *quae omnia nunc intellegit* clause has to be understood as a parenthesislike statement outside
the storyline. This is suggested by the vague back reference *quae omnia* and by *nunc*, although *nunc*
may be used in a past narrative. That this interpretation is correct follows from *illorum
confessionem ... futuras* in the following sentence, which refers to second sentence in this quotation
derisum esse ... Note that the following present form *videt* is easily understood as referring to the
past because of the temporal subordinator *ubi*.

17. First position includes a few instances where, due to hyperbaton, the verbal form is preceded
by a constituent that is not a connective.

As can be seen from table 1, word order is also a discriminating factor in the relationship between historical present and perfect.[18] There are three more distributional differences between these two forms. In the first place historical presents tend to cluster. As will be illustrated also in figure 1 (p. 77 below), isolated instances of the historical present are rare (4 times). In this episode there are two clusters of more than 10 successive historical presents.[19] Clusters of perfects of this length do not occur in this episode, whereas there are 8 instances of isolated perfects. Secondly, sentences and clauses with a present tense are (much) shorter than those with perfect tense forms and, thirdly, they often follow each other asyndetically (27 instances).[20] A good example to illustrate all this is (25):

(25) (Verres realizes that he is in great trouble (*videbat*, imperfect tense)). Consilium *capit* primo stultum, verum tamen clemens. Nauarchos ad se vocari *iubet. Veniunt. Accusat* eos quod eiusmodi de se sermones habuerint, *rogat* ut id facere desistant et in sua quisque dicat se tantum habuisse nautarum, quantum oportuerit, neque quemquam esse dimissum. Illi enimvero se *ostendunt* quod vellet esse facturos. Iste non *procrastinat, advocat* amicos statim; *quaerit* ex iis singillatim quot quisque nautas habuerit; *respondet*[21] unusquisque, ut erat praeceptum; iste in tabulas *refert, obsignat* signis amicorum providens homo, ut contra hoc crimen ... uteretur. Derisum esse credo hominem amentem a suis consiliariis ... et admonitum ... (Cic. *Ver.* 5.101-103)

'His first plan was foolish, but still not cruel. He sent for the captains, and when they appeared, reprimanded them for talking about him as they had; he then requested that each of them would state that he had had the proper number of sailors in his ship, and that no one had been exempted from duty. They, it must be said, signified their readiness to do what he wished. Thereupon without loss of time he had his friends summoned to his presence, and then asked the captains one by one how many sailors he had had; each of them returned the prescribed answer, which Verres caused to be written down and sealed with his friends' seals, with the farsighted intention, we may assume, of using this testimony ... as a defence against the

---

18. For Verb Subject ordering in narrative texts see also Bolkestein (1995a: 42) and Chausserie-Laprée (1969: 350) on this very passage of Cicero.
19. 4x1, 2x2, 2x4, 2x5, 1x7, 1x12, 1x13.
20. Bolkestein (1995a) also notes a correlation between Verb Subject sentences and lack of connnecting devices.
21. *respondet* is the reading of some *recentiores*, accepted by Klotz in his Teubner edition. The older manuscripts have *respondit*, which is accepted by Peterson in his OCT.

charge we are considering. I take it that the fool's own councillors laughed
at him, and pointed out to him ...'

The historical present is much more frequent in this passage than the perfect. As
I said already, some scholars take this in itself as an argument for describing the
historical present as an unmarked tense. Still, the frequency of the historical
present does not make its use plain or ordinary. As we see, there are additional
distributional characteristics which bear similarity to what we know of the use of
the historical present in modern languages (see the discussion on narrative 'peaks'
in Longacre 1983: 25-38, Fleischman 1990: 211 on 'pacing the discourse' and
already Schlicher 1931) and which typically befit salient passages in narrative texts.
See also my visualisation of the use of the tenses in this passage in figure 1 on the
next page.

All this suggests that the historical presents in this text cannot be simply
replaced by perfect forms.[22] If we now turn to the perfect forms, especially to one
of the cases where more perfects occur in succession, it is quite obvious that many
of them cannot be replaced by present forms either.

(26) (After preparations) Egreditur in Centuripina quadriremi Cleomenes e portu;
sequitur Segestana navis ... Tam diu in imperio suo classem iste praetor
diligens *vidit* quam diu convivium eius flagitiosissimum *praetervecta est*; ipse
autem, qui visus multis diebus non esset, tum se tamen in conspectum nautis
paulisper *dedit. Stetit* soleatus praetor populi Romani cum pallio purpureo
tunicaque talari muliercula nixus in litore. Nam hoc istum vestitu Siculi
civesque Romani permulti saepe *viderunt*[23] (Cic. *Ver.* 5.86)
'Cleomenes sailed out of the harbour in the Centuripan ship, a quadrireme,
followed by the ship of Segesta ... All that our governor saw of this fleet that
was under his authority was during the time it sailed past the scene of his
shameful carousals; he himself had been invisible for many days, but on this
occasion he did for a few moments show himself to his sailors. That Roman
governor stood there on the shore in slippers, wearing a purple Greek cloak
and a long-skirted tunic, and leaning on one of his women; and often enough
before that had any number of Sicilians and Romans citizens seen him in this
costume.'

---

22. Replacement of the present is certainly not possible where in subordinate clauses present
consecutio is observed, as with *habuerint* and *dicat* in this passage. There are also cases where the
present is similar to an imperfect as far as background status is concerned (various contributions
by Kravar, among these 1971).
23. I follow Klotz' Teubner text in reading *nam* (Ernesti instead of *iam*, codd.) and *viderunt* (codd.).
Peterson, in his OCT, keeps *iam* and follows Benedictus in reading *viderant*.

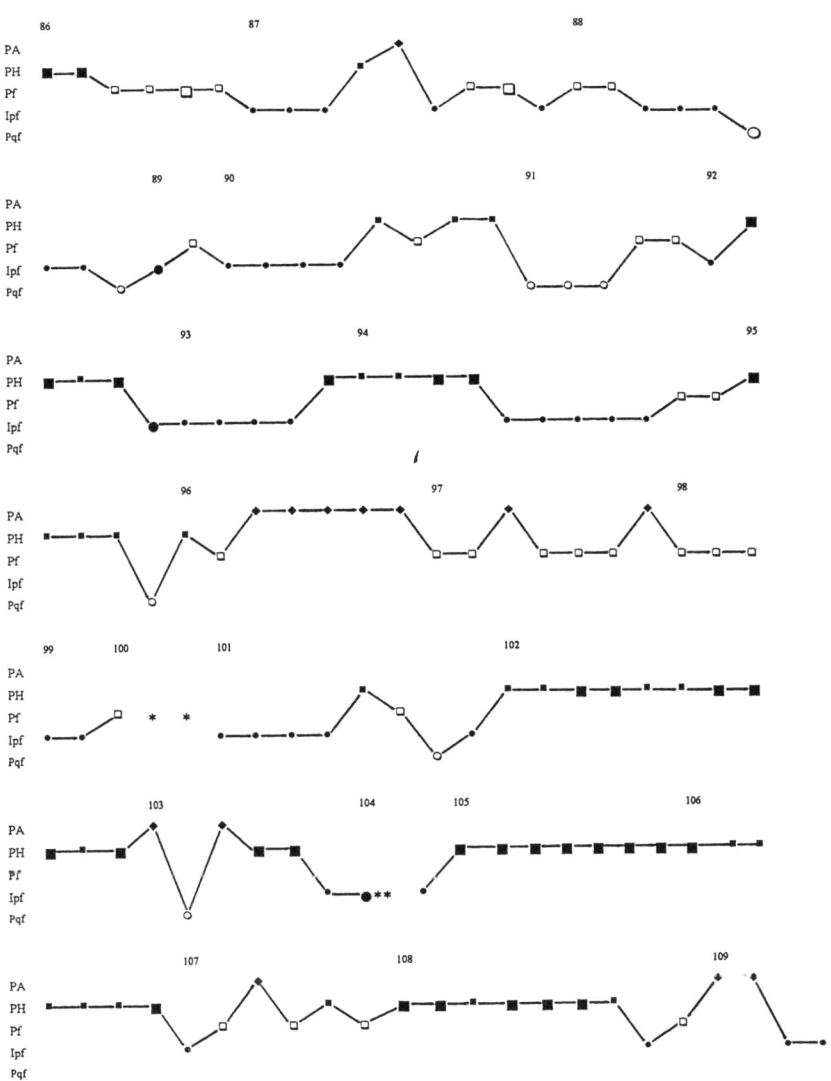

Larger dots and blocks indicate clause initial tense forms
* historical infinitives
** direct discourse

Figure 1: The use of the tenses in Cic. *Ver.* 5.86-109

In the passage quoted under (26) the sentence with *vidit* is a comment of Cicero outside the storyline about Verres' general practice (*in imperio suo*) (note also the evaluative adjective *flagitiosissimum*). The final sentence with *viderunt* is also a statement outside the storyline, whatever reading we choose. In this type of comments about past events that do not form part of the storyline the perfect cannot be replaced by a present tense. Only truly narrative perfects may be replaced by present tense forms, but, as I have tried to show, on condition that the speaker thinks it is appropriate[24] in the order of the story, and in combination with a number of other — syntactic — features.[25] The function of the narrative perfects, which are by no means always easy to distinguish from 'authorial' perfects, seems to be to switch from the speaker's situation to the past and back. In this way both uses (authorial and narrative)[26] are in accordance with the function of the perfect in the tense system, presenting states of affairs as anterior to, finished or ended before, the speech situation.[27]

It is a well-known fact that the Roman historians and epic poets frequently use the present as a narrative tense and sometimes even as the main narrative tense.[28] The high frequency is to some extent caused by the fact that the present is not only used to report ongoing actions, but also to give background information, which is one of the main functions of the imperfect.[29] However, Chausserie-Laprée (1969: 372) and others have shown that in certain identical syntactic configurations (for example the '*cum* inversum' construction) the present and the perfect seem to be exchangeable in the *cum*-clause. It is quite possible that

24. "Evidently conversational narrators have a tendency to slip into the historical present at points in their talk where there is some reason for a remembered event or state to be expressed in a way that more closely resembles the immediate mode, a strategy likely to be most appropriate at, or shortly before, the climax of a narrative." (Chafe 1994: 209-210).
25. As a consequence, the proportion of historical presents among the truly narrative past tenses is even higher than table 1 suggests. It is extremely likely that the syntactic phenomena referred to were combined with a specific intonational contour, speed, volume, pauses to create tension, etc.
26. What I have called 'authorial' and 'narrative' perfects corresponds roughly to distinctions like 'present perfect' (sometimes called 'perfective perfect' or 'perfectum praesens') and 'historical perfect' (sometimes called 'aoristic perfect') (Pinkster 1990: 229-232). The notion 'authorial' (German 'auktorial') stems from narratological studies in the tradition of Stanzel. It is also used by Klug (1992), Kroon & Rose (1996), and Kroon (this vol.).
27. For a survey of the situations in which a perfect is preferred see Schlicher (1931: 56-59) and Chausserie-Laprée (1969: 371-373, 554, n. 1).
28. Quinn (1968: 93, note 1), for example, states that in Virgil's time the use of the historical present had become a stylistic mannerism.
29. For the use of the present in situations in which the imperfect is also possible see Kravar (1971). Mellet (1985) makes no distinction among the historical presents between those that resemble imperfect forms and those that resemble perfect forms in their behaviour. Dragonetti (1981: 72) has the following figures from Apuleius' *Psyche* story (main clauses, direct speech excluded):

imperfect	64	present ('impf.')	88
perfect	101	present ('perf.')	145

the rules for using the present and perfect as narrative tenses in these types of texts differ from the use in conversation and direct address discussed above.[30] The fact that the hearer or reader knows from the beginning that the narrated events are situated in the past creates the possibility for the author to exploit the tenses for other purposes than locating events in time. Often there is another major difference, *viz.* a difference in length of the narrative. This creates the need for the author to introduce variations of various types, and for this purpose, too, the tenses may be used in non-locating functions.[31] However, Caesar, Livy, Sallust and Tacitus use the present with varying frequency and not as often clusterwise as we saw it in Cicero. Nevertheless, in these authors as well there are distributional differences between the present and the perfect. The present seems to be preferred, for example, when an important advance is made in the progress of events (cf. Klug 1992).[32]

Conversely, there are also situations in these types of text in which a present is dispreferred or inappropriate. The present is dispreferred and possibly excluded in author comments outside the storyline as in (27) and (28):

(27) (After Iuno's words)
      Olli (*sensit* enim simulata mente locutam,
      quo regnum Italiae Libycas averteret oras)
      sic contra est *ingressa* Venus: (Verg. *A.* 4.105-107)
      'To her — for she knew that with feigned purpose she had spoken, to turn
      the empire from Italy to Libya's coasts — Venus thus began in reply:'

(28) (Psyche's father consults the oracle of Apollo in Miletus)
      Sed Apollo, quamquam Graecus et Ionicus, propter Milesiae conditorem sic
      Latina sorte *respondit*: (Apul. *Met.* 4.32)
      'But Apollo, though he were a Grecian of the country of Ionia, yet for the
      sake of him that telleth this Milesian tale, gave answer in Latin verse, the
      sense whereof was this:'

In (27) *sensit* occurs in an author comment, as appears from *enim*. This explains why the perfect is used, not the fact that the situation described is about gods, as Von Albrecht (1970) suggests. In (28) the perfect is not used because it is

---

30. The use of the tenses in literary fiction may be different from their use in (literary) historical narrative. See Vuillaume (1990). In Antiquity, the two types were probably not so far apart (cf. Klug 1992: 10).
31. The best discussion of all this can be found in Fleischman (1990).
32. He calls the present an 'Initiativtempus' (Klug 1992: 35) used for "vorwärtsstrebende oder verändernde Handlungsinitiative" (*ibid.*, 101).

"introduisant l'oracle fatal qui va bouleverser la destinée de Psyché" (Mellet 1985: 150). Rather it is "The most striking, one might almost say blatant, manifestation of the authorial presence" (Kenney 1990: 23).

The present seems to be inappropriate in descriptions of extreme cruelty, such as the killing of Priam in Virgil *A*. 2.550-553 (four coordinated perfects on a row). In using the perfect Aeneas reports the events as an objective outsider, creating distance, and in this way stressing the gruesome outcome of the events (cf. Quinn 1968: 93, note 1). In these types of text, too, there are limitations on the use of the present.

5. Conclusion

I have tried to show that for each of the types of situations where the present seems to be used or is used without referring to the speaker's now there are certain restrictions and conditions which distinguish the present from other tenses. The reverse holds as well. The present cannot be substituted for other tenses in all situations. From this I conclude that the present has its own place in the tense system with a specific, 'positive', semantic value of its own: 'presenting a state of affairs as contemporaneous with the speech situation', rather then regarding it as a tense indicating as its basic meaning 'atemporality'.

It has been observed by Moralejo (1988) and others (for example Fleischman 1990: 53-54) that in the classical theory of markedness the fact that the present tense has a specific function of its own is not incompatible with its being the unmarked member in the set of tenses. In its 'minus-interpretation' (Fleischman) the present may specifically refer to the speech situation. This may be so. However, in order to describe the specific effects of, for example, the historical present, it has to be assumed in the theory of markedness that the atemporal present is used to refer to past events while keeping its 'minus-interpretation' 'here and now'. For me, this is one step too much.[33]

---

33. I would like to thank Daan den Hengst, Machtelt Bolkestein, and Caroline Kroon for their critical observations on a preliminary version of this paper and Mathieu de Bakker for his assistance.

Bibliography

Albrecht, M. von
  1970 Zu Vergil's Erzähltechnik: Beobachtungen zum Tempusgebrauch in der Aeneis. *Glotta* 48, 219-229
Bennett, C.E.
  1910 *Syntax of Early Latin. I: The Verb*. Boston (=Hildesheim, Olms, 1966)
Bolkestein, A. M.
  1995a Functions of the verb-subject order in Latin. *Sprachtypologische Universalien Forschung (STUF)* 48, 32-43
  1995b Questions about questions. In: Longrée, Dominique (ed.) *De USU*. Louvain/Paris: Peeters, p. 59-70
Chafe, W.
  1994 *Discourse, Consciousness and Time. The Flow and Displacement of Conscious Experience in Speaking and Writing*. Chicago: University Press
Chausserie-Laprée, J.-P.
  1969 *L'expression narrative chez les historiens latins*. Paris: De Boccard
Dragonetti, M.
  1981 Uso dei tempi e degli aspetti verbali a fini stilistici nella favola di "Amore e Psiche" di Apuleio. *Aevum* 55, 69-79
Fleischman, S.
  1990 *Tense and Narrativity*. London: Routledge
Heinze, R.
  1924 Zum Gebrauch des *Praesens historicum* im Altlatein. In: *Streitberg Festgabe*. Leipzig: Markert & Petters, p. 121-132
Hofmann, J.B.
  1950[3] *Lateinische Umgangssprache*. Heidelberg: Winter
Kenney, E.J.
  1990 *Apuleius. Cupid & Psyche*. Edited by E.J. Kenney. Cambridge: University Press
Klein, W.
  1994 *Time in Language*. London: Routledge
Klug, W.
  1992 *Erzählstruktur als Kunstform. Studien zur künstlerischen Funktion der Erzähltempora im Lateinischen und im Griechischen*. Heidelberg: Manutius Verlag
Kravar, M.
  1971 Quousque über das historische Präsens. *Živa Antika* 21, 155-158
Kroon, C.H.M.
  1995 *Discourse Particles in Latin: A Study of* nam, enim, autem, vero *and* at. Amsterdam: Gieben
Kroon, C.H.M. & P. Rose
  1996 Atrociter corruptus? The use of 'narrative' tenses in Ammianus Marcellinus' *Res Gestae*. In: R. Risselada *et al.* (eds) *On Latin. Linguistic and literary Studies in Honour of Harm Pinkster*. Amsterdam: Gieben, p. 71-89

Kühner, R. & C. Stegmann
    1912-1914   *Ausführliche Grammatik der lateinischen Sprache. II: Satzlehre* (2 vols).
                Hannover: Hahnsche Buchhandlung
Labov, W.
    1972   *The Language in the Inner City.* Philadelphia: University of Pennsylvania Press
Lodge, G.
    1924   *Lexicon Plautinum.* Leipzig: Teubner
Longacre, R.E.
    1983   *The Grammar of Discourse.* New York/London: Plenum Press
Mellet, S.
    1985   Présent de narration et parfait dans le conte de Psyché. *Revue des Études
           Latines* 63, 148-160
Mellet, S., N.-D. Joffre & G. Serbat
    1994   *Grammaire fondamentale du latin: Le signifié du verbe.* Louvain/Paris: Peeters
Moralejo, J.L.
    1988   Le présent: un temps pour toutes saisons. *L'Information Grammaticale* 38,
           28-32
Myhill, J.
    1992   *Typological Discourse Analysis.* Oxford: Blackwell
Petersmann, H.
    1973   *T. Maccius Plautus, Stichus. Einleitung, Text, Kommentar.* Heidelberg: Winter
    1977   *Petrons urbane Prosa. Untersuchungen zu Sprache und Text (Syntax).* Wien:
           Verlag der Österreichischen Akademie der Wissenschaften
Pinkster, H.
    1983   Tempus, Aspect and *Aktionsart* in Latin (Recent trends 1961-1981). *Aufstieg
           und Niedergang der römischen Welt* 29:1, 270-319
    1990   *Latin Syntax and Semantics.* London: Routledge
Quinn, K.
    1968   *Virgil's Aeneid. A Critical Description.* London: Routledge
Recanati, F.
    1995   Le présent épistolaire: une perspective cognitive. *L'Information Grammaticale*
           66, 38-44
Schlicher, J.J.
    1931   Historical tenses and their functions in Latin. *Classical Philology* 26, 46-59
Serbat, G.
    1976   Das Präsens im lateinischen Tempusystem. *Zeitschrift für Vergleichende
           Sprachforschung* 90, 200-221
    1988   Le prétendu "présent de l'indicatif": une forme non-déictique du verbe.
           L'Information Grammaticale 38, 32-36
Sjögren, H.
    1906   *Zum Gebrauch des Futurums im Altlateinischen.* Uppsala: Akademiska
           Bokhandeln / Leipzig: Harassowitz
Szantyr, A.
    1965   *Lateinische Syntax und Stilistik.* München: Beck

Töchterle, K.

1994 *Lucius Annaeus Seneca Oedipus. Kommentar mit Einleitung, Text und Übersetzung*. Heidelberg: Winter

Touratier, C.

1994 *Syntaxe latine*. Louvain/Paris: Peeters

1996 Les temps dans un récit (Virgile, *Ecloga* 7.1-20). In: R. Risselada *et al.* (eds) *On Latin. Linguistic and literary Studies in Honour of Harm Pinkster*. Amsterdam: Gieben, p. 163-172

Vuillaume, M.

1990 *Grammaire temporelle des récits*. Paris: Les Éditions de Minuit

Weinrich, H.

1964 *Tempus. Besprochene und erzählte Welt*. Stuttgart: Kohlhammer

Wisse, J.

1996 The presence of Zeno. The date of Philodemus' *On Rhetoric* and the use of the 'citative' and 'reproducing' present in Latin and Greek. In: R. Risselada *et al.* (eds) *On Latin. Linguistic and literary Studies in Honour of Harm Pinkster*. Amsterdam: Gieben, p. 173-202

Tandem and *postremo*: two of a kind?

Rodie Risselada

Descriptions of tandem *tend to centre on the emotions (protest, anger, impatience) which this Latin discourse particle is usually taken to convey. In this paper an alternative account is proposed, which is based on a contrastive analysis of* tandem *and* postremo. *These two discourse particles share a basic semantic value of 'finality' or 'ultimateness', but they differ as to the question in what respect they mark their host units as 'final'. While* postremo *is a straightforward connective particle, which serves to indicate that its host unit is the last member of a series of events that are all explicitly described in the context, or the last member of a coherent sequence of explicit discourse units,* tandem *serves to evaluate its host unit (an event, a communicative action, or the content of a speech act) as 'final' or 'ultimate' in comparison with the speaker's implicit expectations. As such,* tandem *is not a connective, but an evaluative particle, which links its host unit with attitudes and beliefs that are entertained in the communicative situation. On the basis of this approach we can account in a unified way for the quite divergent ways in which* tandem *is used in Latin texts.*

1. Introduction[1]

One of the best-known instances of *tandem* is found in the famous opening line of Cicero's first Catilinarian speech:

(1)   Quo usque *tandem* abutere, Catilina, patientia nostra? (Cic. *Catil.* 1.1)
       '*In heaven's name*, Catiline, how long will you take advantage of our
       forebearance?'

Tandem is usually associated with the emotions — impatience, protest, anger, despair — which Cicero conveyed so effectively in the powerful opening of this speech. The *Oxford Latin Dictionary* (*OLD*), for instance, states (*sub* 1b) that in instances such as (1) *tandem* is "used to emphasize [a question], expressing a strong sense of protest or impatience", and gives as translations 'really, I ask you, after all'. The Loeb translation 'in heaven's name', quoted under (1), points in the same

1. This research (project 300-172-016) was supported by the Foundation for Language, Speech and Logic, which is funded by the Netherlands Organisation for Scientific Research, NWO. I am very grateful to my Amsterdam colleagues, especially Caroline Kroon and Harm Pinkster, for their valuable comments on various earlier versions of this paper.

direction. Impatience is, furthermore, mentioned in commentaries, cf. e.g. Haury (1969) on *tandem* in this passage: "Ici impatience d'être soulagé, mais le soulagement même dans l'exorde de *Cat.* 2: *Tandem aliquando*".[2]

However, if this view of *tandem* as a mere expression of protest or impatience in instances such as (1) is correct, one wonders how this usage relates to the other usages of *tandem*, in which the emotions conveyed are not necessarily always so negative and *tandem* has quite different functions. There is, first of all, a well-known group of instances (discussed in the *OLD* under 2) in which *tandem* conveys the speaker's relief that a particular expected, but delayed event has 'finally' or 'at last' taken place. An example is the opening line of Cicero's second Catilinarian:

(2)   *Tandem* aliquando, Quirites, L. Catilinam furentem audacia, scelus anhelan-
       tem, pestem patriae nefarie molientem, vobis atque huic urbi ferro flamma-
       que minitantem ex urbe vel eiecimus vel emisimus vel ipsum egredientem
       verbis prosecuti sumus. Abiit, excessit, evasit, erupit. (Cic. *Catil.* 2.1)
       '*At long last*, citizens, we have cast out of the city or dismissed or said
       farewell to Lucius Catiline, as he departed, blazing wih audacity, breathing
       forth crime, wickedly plotting the destruction of this country, threatening
       you and this city with sword and fire. He has gone, departed, escaped, flung
       himself out.'

Although it is not impossible to connect the latter case in an intuitive way with the former, e.g. along the lines suggested by Haury's comment quoted above, the difference between the two types of cases in emotions conveyed (impatient protest versus relief) is remarkable.

However, there are also instances in which the conveyance of emotions does not seem to be a primary function of *tandem* at all, as in the following utterance (the transition to a new discourse topic in Cicero's defence of Milo), in which *tandem* is used to indicate that the 'answer' anounced will be based on all relevant considerations:

(3)   Videamus nunc id, quod caput est, locus ad insidias ille ipse, ubi congressi
       sunt, utri *tandem* fuerit aptior. (Cic. *Mil.* 53)
       'Let us now look to the crux of the whole matter, and see which party had
       after all (or: all things considered) the better position for an ambush in the
       spot where the meeting actually occurred.'

---

2. Similarly Richter-Eberhard-Nohl (1912): "eig. der Ausdruck erfüllter Erwartung (2,1), in rhetorischen Fragen 'denn'". Cf. also Halm-Sternkopf (1916): "'denn eigentlich', 'in aller Welt' ...".

Then, there are still other cases which, although they may involve some note of impatience, differ quite clearly from instances such as (1). An example is (4), in which *tandem* is used twice in combination with *sed* (which marks 'discontinuity' here, cf. Kroon 1995: 70; 86) to introduce a new and potentially final stage in the speaker's train of thought:

(4)   (Pinacium is on his way to bring his mistress important news; he is urging himself on to run as quickly as he can, when suddenly he changes his mind; after having elaborated on this new course of action, he again changes his mind)

Sed *tandem*, opinor, aequiust eram mihi esse supplicem   290
atque oratores mittere ad me donaque ex auro et quadrigas
qui vehar, nam pedibus ire non queo. (...)
Sed *tandem* quom recogito, qui potuit scire haec scire me?   303
non enim possum quin revortar, quin loquar, quin edissertem
eramque ex maerore eximam (...) (Pl. *St.* 290-303)
'But *after all*, methinks, 't were more fitting for mistress to petition me and send me envoys and gifts of gold and a four-horse chariot for transportation. No indeed, travel afoot is not for me. (...) But *after all*, on second thoughts, how could she know that I know this? Ah well, I see I must return, speak out, unfold it all, and sweep away her sorrow.'

Finally, there is a group of instances in which *tandem* pertains to an event which, contrary to cases such as (2), is totally unexpected. Most commonly, this usage of *tandem* involves negative emotions, cf. (5), but it may also involve mere incredulity, as in (6):

(5)   (The *meretrix* Erotium is angry because her lover Menaechmus demands that she returns a present)
ER: (...) Tu huc post hunc diem pedem intro non feres, ne frustra sis; (...)
nisi feres argentum, frustra me ductare non potes.
Aliam posthac invenito quam habeas frustratui.
ME: Nimis iracunde hercle *tandem*. (Pl. *Men.* 692-696)
'You shall not set foot in this house after today, don't fool yourself. (...) you can bring along ready money, or else you can't lead me along like a fool. After this you just find somebody else to fool. # Oh gad, *now, really*, you're too testy.'

(6)   (A servant and a cook are discussing the avarice of the neighbour)
       SE: (...) Pumex non aeque est aridus atque hic est senex.
       CO: Ain *tandem*? SE: Ita esse ut dixi. (Pl. *Aul.* 297-298)
       'You couldn't squeeze as much out of that old chap as you could out of a
       pumice stone. # Oh, *really now!* # That's a fact.'

This brief and by no means exhaustive impression of the versatility of *tandem*
raises the question what exactly is the function of this particle in each of these
usages, and how one could account for the similarities and the differences between
them.

The few overall accounts of *tandem* that are available[3] all assume at least two
different 'meanings', one that can be paraphrased by 'at last, finally' ('endlich';
'enfin') and a second one that is usually paraphrased by 'really' ('wirklich') and
which is defined in the OLD in terms of impatience and protest (see above, *ad* ex.
1). The aim of this paper is to outline a more unified account, which is based on
a fairly constant basic meaning of 'finality' or 'ultimateness', which interacts in a
number of different ways with the utterances and contexts in which *tandem* is
used. This account will be presented in sections 3 - 6. It is based on a corpus of ca
250 instances, taken from Plautus, Terence, Cicero, Lucretius, Livy, Virgil, Pliny,
Petronius and Apuleius.

However, as a first step towards a clearer view of *tandem*, I will start with
a brief overview of the functions of a discourse particle that also expresses 'finality'
and that is often considered to resemble *tandem* in some of its uses, viz. *postremo*.[4]
This analysis of *postremo*, given in section 2, not only serves as a contrastive background which will enable us to characterize *tandem*'s discourse functions more
clearly (cf. section 3), but it forms also a good startingpoint to introduce a number
of concepts on which my account of *tandem* is based.

In the last section, I will briefly return to the function of *tandem* in (1). I
will argue that the contribution of *tandem* to the emotional impact of this opening
line is much more indirect than is usually assumed, and that the alleged emotional

---

3. The *Oxford Latin Dictionary*; Langen (1880: 88-91, *ad* Pl. *As.* 176); Petersmann (1973, *ad* Pl. *St.*
765). Note that Hand (1829-1845) does not discuss *tandem* and that it has not yet been dealt with
by the *Thesaurus Linguae Latinae.*
       In addition, some authors (e.g Donatus *ad* Ter. *Eun.* 1055, followed by Ussing 1875, *ad* Pl.
As. 176 and Woytek 1982, *ad* Pl. *Rud.* 468; see note 27) propose an additional meaning, in which
tandem equals *saltem*, while others assume (cf. the next note) that *tandem* is sometimes used to
conclude enumerations or lists.
4. Cf. e.g. the *TLL* s.v. *postremo*, p. 217, l. 66, and the similar treatment in the *OLD* of part of the
instances of *postremo* (*sub* 3) and *tandem* (*sub* 2). Furthermore, Krebs & Schmalz (1907, s.v. *tandem*)
and Gutierrez Galinda (1989) also seem to assume that *tandem*, just like *postremo* or *denique*, can
be used to introduce the last item of a series.

value is largely due to other properties of the utterance as a whole and to its verbal and, especially, its non-verbal context.

2. Background: the clear-cut case of *postremo*

Together with expressions such as *primo, deinde, praeterea* and *denique, postremo* belongs to the category of so-called sequential discourse marker. Sequential markers serve (i) to indicate that the text unit which they introduce (their 'host unit')[5] does not stand on its own, but forms part of a sequence of similar units, and (ii) to mark the position of their host unit within this sequence.[6] While *primo* indicates that its host unit constitutes the first part of a sequence, and *deinde* and *praeterea* introduce units that form a sequel to other units, the function of *postremo* is to indicate that its host unit closes the sequence to which it belongs. A number of sequential markers are combined in (7), where they mark the various stages of a career:[7]

(7)   modo consul quondam, is *deinde* primus erat civitatis; *tum* proficitur in Asiam; *deinde* hostis et exul est dictus; *post* imperator, et *postremo* <VII> factus est consul (*Rhet. Her.* 4.68)
        'just recently consul, *next* he was first man of the state; *then* he sets out for Asia; *next* he is declared a public enemy and exiled; *after that* he is made imperator and *finally* consul for the seventh time'

---

5. The term 'host unit' is taken from Kroon (1995). The host unit of a discourse marker, is "the particular stretch of text to which the force of the particle involved pertains. The concept of 'unit' or 'host unit' is not necessarily coextensive with the concept of 'clause': it stands rather for a pragmatically (and not formally) determined stretch of text, and may apply to any kind of information-conveying text segment, ranging from single words to a cluster of several sentences." (Kroon 1995: 35, n. 3).
6. Cf. Kühner-Stegmann, who describe the expressions involved as "Ausdrücke, die eine Reihenfolge ... bezeignen" (K-St. II, 69). 'Anreihung' is regarded by them as a form of 'kopulative Beiordnung'. Interesting is also the definition given by Nøjgaard (1992: 241) of the corresponding expressions in French (which he calls *les relationnels sériels: d'abord, ensuite, enfin, (et puis), finalement*, etc.): "Les relationnels sériels servent à couper la progression discursive en segments ordonnés. Ils signalent que les arguments se succèdent dans un ordre fixé, attribuant ainsi une valeur argumentative à la succession même. (..) Ils ne nous informent pas sur le statut logique de l'argument introduit, mais nous disent seulement qu'il faut interpréter celui-ci comme une partie d'un ensemble progressif."
7. This 'invented example' is given by the author of the *Rhetorica ad Herennium* as an example of *brevitas*.

2.1 Discourse markers versus adjuncts

As to their form, sequential discourse markers can be analyzed as temporal adverbs. Functionally, however, they should be distinguished from adverbs that function as regular temporal adjuncts (e.g. *quondam, antea, sero, nunc*)[8] and serve to indicate at which moment the event described in the utterance obtains. As opposed to the latter, sequential markers are not syntactically integrated in their hosting clause nor do they form part of its propositional content. Instead, their function should be analyzed in terms of the structure of the surrounding discourse. Thus, in (7), *postremo* does not answer the question "when did he become consul", as would be the case if it were a temporal adjunct, but serves to introduce the answer to "what was the last stage of his career?", a question which ensues from the fact that the utterance forms part of a larger sequence. The 'extra-clausal' status of *postremo* (and other sequential markers) is also indicated by the size of its host units: in Lucretius, for instance, *postremo* is regularly used to introduce a whole paragraph which constitutes a single argument in an argumentative sequence.

Further indications for the discourse marker status of *postremo* are the fact that it cannot occur in isolation (e.g. as an answer to a question), that it is never topic or focus in the utterance to which it belongs or involved in a contrast, and that it cannot be modified, as is e.g. possible for *nunc* and *post* when they are used as an adjunct (cf. *multo post; iam nunc*, etc.).[9]

2.2 Levels of discourse

Lexica and dictionaries usually list a number of different meanings of *postremo*. It seems, however, more adequate to assume just one basic meaning (viz. marking that its host unit does not stand on its own, but forms the final item in a sequence) and to explain the variety of uses as resulting from differences in the nature of the sequences to which *postremo*'s host units may belong.

A basic distinction is usually made (e.g. in the *TLL s.v.*; cf. also Kühner-Stegmann II, 69) between 'temporal' uses and 'argumentative' uses. In the former

---

8. Note that *nunc* can also be used as a discourse marker. Risselada (1996) discusses a number of criteria to distinguish between its uses as a temporal adjunct and as a discourse marker. *Post*, which is a sequential discourse marker in (4), likewise combines an adjunct and a marker use.

9. It should be noted that there are a few isolated instances in which *postremo* is used as a temporal adjunct at sentence level ('at the end', 'at the latest moment'), cf. Cato *Agr.* 131. This isolated 'adjunct use' of *postremo*, which is normally fulfilled by *postremum* (cf. the almost verbally similar example in Cato *Agr.* 50.2), will not be discussed in this paper. It is, however, not problematic to link the basic meaning of the discourse particle *postremo* with *postremo*'s full lexical meaning as a temporal adjunct.

type of use *postremo* signals that the event described in its host unit closes a series of connected events, as in (7) above and in (8):

(8)   *Primo* incaute se invehentes Masinissa excipiebat; *mox* plures simul conferti porta effusi aequaverant certamen; *postremo*, iam omnis equitatus proelio cum adesset, sustineri ultra nequiere. (Liv. 29.34.12)
      '*At first*, as they rashly charged, Masinissa would meet their attack; *later* larger numbers dashing out of a gate in a mass, had made it an even combat; *finally*, when all their cavalry was engaged, they could no longer be withstood.'

In the latter, the so-called argumentative type of use, *postremo* indicates that its host unit forms the last item of a coherent sequence of discourse units. This sequence may be an enumeration:

(9)   confecta labore volneribus *postremo* aetate corpora (Liv. 5.10.9)
      'bodies worn out by hard labour, wounds, and, *finally*, age'

but it may also consist of a series of arguments, as in (10). In this passage from his first speech against Verres, Cicero lists a number of arguments why this trial is so crucial. The penultimate argument is introduced by *deinde*, the last one by *postremo*:[10]

(10) Hoc est iudicium in quo vos de reo, populus Romanus de vobis iudicabit. In hoc homine statuetur possitne senatoribus iudicantibus homo nocentissimus pecuniosissimusque damnari. *Deinde* est eius modi reus in quo homine (...). *Postremo* ego causam sic agam, iudices, eius modi res, ita notas, ita (...) proferam, ut nemo a vobis ut istum absolvatis per gratiam conetur contendere. (Cic. *Ver.* 47-48)
      'It is the present trial in which, even as you will pass your verdict upon the prisoner, so the people of Rome will pass its verdict upon yourselves. It is this man's case that will determine whether, with a court composed of Senators, the condemnation of a very guilty and very rich man can possibly occur. *And further*, the prisoner is such that he (...). *And lastly*, gentlemen, I shall so handle this case, I shall put before you facts of such a kind, so

10. Another example is *Rhet. Her.* 3.38-39, where the various arguments are also each introduced by a sequential marker. Often, however, only the last argument is marked, by *postremo*, cf. e.g. Liv. 5.24.10.

notorious, so (...) that nobody will seek to urge you to acquit this man as a personal favour.'

The distinction between the 'temporal' and 'argumentative' uses of *postremo* coincides with a distinction that has been made in a more general way in Kroon's (1995) study of Latin discourse particles. According to Kroon, discourse particles "... fit their host unit into a wider perspective, which may be the surrounding verbal context and its implications, or the communicative situation in which the text is integrated" (1995: 35). Their function is to signal the various 'coherence relations' that may obtain between their host units and elements in the verbal or non-verbal context. In order to account for the different types of coherence relations that can be indicated by discourse particles, she distinguishes three 'levels of discourse' on which coherence relations may obtain:

(i)   the *representational* level, which concerns the (relations between) extra-linguistic events that are described ('represented') in utterances;

(ii)   the *presentational* level, which concerns the way in which speakers organize their discourse and 'stage' information units with respect to one another;

(iii)   the *interactional* level, which pertains to units of discourse in connection with the ongoing interaction between speaker and addressee.

Discourse particles that have a function on the representational level may indicate for instance causal, consequential or temporal relations between events in the extra-linguistic world that are described by the speaker. These representational relations must be distinguished from the so-called presentational (or discourse organizational) relations, which can also be marked by discourse particles, such as the relation between a claim and its arguments, the relation between a question or directive and its motivation, and relations of a preparatory or elaborating nature. Presentational coherence relations do not primarily pertain to the content of utterances, but to their status as units of discourse within the structure of the surrounding discourse. Discourse particles that function on the third, interactional level of discourse, finally, indicate coherence relations between a unit of discourse and the communicative intentions, beliefs and attitudes of the speaker and the addressee.

    The distinction between the representational and the presentational level of discourse is relevant to distinguish between the two ways in which sequential markers such as *postremo* can be used: the so-called 'temporal use' belongs to the representational level, while the 'argumentative use' pertains to the presentational (or 'organizational') level of discourse. Both 'uses' share an invariable common 'basic meaning', because in all of its uses *postremo* indicates that its host unit is the last unit of a given sequence. They differ, however, as to the nature of the sequence involved, which is extra-linguistic and strictly temporal when *postremo* functions as a representational discourse marker, and textual and enumerative or listlike when *postremo* functions as a presentational marker. The third, interactional level of discourse, is not relevant for *postremo*. It will, however, turn out to be very relevant for the analysis of *tandem*.

Postremo is, in itself, neutral as to the structure of the sequence to which its host unit belongs. In the examples given up to this moment, the sequences involved consist of units that are roughly equivalent. In some cases the unit introduced by *postremo* may happen to be the most salient or important one, but that is not due to the presence of *postremo*. It is a common rhetorical strategy that speakers save the most important or salient item of an enumeration or argumentative sequence for the end, and this strategy may be chosen regardless of whether or not *postremo* is used.

However, there are also instances in which the unit introduced by *postremo* is not on a par with the preceding units, but is of a more general nature and summarizes the sequence as a whole:

(11)   ad recte, honeste, laudabiliter, *postremo* ad bene vivendum (Cic. *Tusc.* 5.12)
        'for living rightly, honourably, praiseworthily, and *in a word* for leading a good life'

Occasionally, *postremo* is even used, at the presentational level, to introduce an ultimate argumentative step of a different nature. An example is (12). The *senex* Demipho wants to re-open the discussion as to whether or not his son can be forced to marry a particular girl just because this girl claims to be a relative of them. Phormio first rejects the reopening of this discussion on the basis of a principle of Roman law: *actum ne agas*. When Demipho does not accept this, Phormio protests (*ineptis* 'you are crazy'), and then puts forward a quite different point as his ultimate argument, introduced by *postremo*:

(12)   PH: Ohe,
        "actum" aiunt "ne agas". DE: Non agam? Immo haud desinam
        donec perfecero hoc. PH: Ineptis. DE: Sine modo.
        PH: *Postremo* tecum nil rei nobis, Demipho, est:
        tuos est damnatus gnatus, non tu; nam tua
        praeterierat iam ducendi aetas. (Ter. *Ph.* 418-423)
        'Oh dear! "settled once, settled forever", as the saying goes # Settled forever?
        I will never rest till I have unsettled it # Idle talk! never you mind! # *As a*
        last word, with you, Demipho, we have no concern; the order of the court
        dealt with your son, not with you: in fact you had already passed the age of
        matrimony.'

In this type of case, the host unit of *postremo* does not add just another, similar type of argument to a previously presented (series of) argument(s), but it replaces preceding arguments altogether, by a completely different, ultimate argument. This replacive relation of the host unit vis-à-vis what precedes is, however, not in itself indicated by *postremo*. As in the other instances, *postremo* just signals that its host unit forms the last item of a series of units that are somehow connected. In (12) they are connected by their both being arguments in favour of a particular behaviour, but they happen to be arguments that do not reinforce, but replace each other.

2.3 Illocutionary force of the host unit

As a marker of representational sequences *postremo* is exclusively used in host units that have an assertive function, to introduce the last stage in the sequential description of a complex event. When it has a function on the presentational level, *postremo* may occur in host units that have other illocutionary functions as well, although these are relatively infrequent as compared to assertive host units. The illocutionary function of the host unit has no influence on *postremo*'s function. Its function (viz. to signal that its host unit forms the last item in a sequence) is exactly the same regardless of whether the sequence involved consists of assertive speech acts (as in the examples given above), directives (cf. 13) or rhetorical questions (cf. 14):

(13)   CH: Dic convenisse, egisse te de nuptiis.
       ME: Dicam; quid *deinde*? CH: me facturum esse omnia,
       generum placere; *postremo* etiam, si voles,
       desponsam quoque esse dicito. (Ter. *Hau.* 863-866)
       'Tell him you have seen me and proposed the match. # I will, *and then*? #
       Say that I am entirely agreeable, that I like the son-in-law; *finally*, if you
       want, you even may say there is a betrothal.'

(14)   DE: Redde operam mihi.
       Cur hoc ego ex te quaeram? Aut cur miniter tibi
       propterea quod me non scientem feceris?
       Aut cur *postremo* filio suscenseam,
       patres ut faciunt ceteri? (Pl. *As.* 46-50)
       'Now listen to me: why should I ask you about this? Or threaten you
       because you haven't informed me? Or, *finally*, why should I fly into a rage
       at my son, as other fathers do?'

2.4 Summary

The picture that arises out of the preceding sections is straightforward. *Postremo* is a sequential marker that indicates that its host unit forms the last item of a sequence. This sequence may consist of a series of connected extra-linguistic events that are described in the discourse (representational *postremo)* or of a series of coherent discourse units (presentational *postremo)*, most often an enumeration or a series of arguments for a particular argumentative position. *Postremo* does not fulfil any discourse functions on the interactional level of discourse.

 Postremo is, both on the representational and the presentational level, neutral with respect to the relationship between the various units of the sequence involved. This sequence may be a listlike, enumerative relationship or a more asymetrical relationship, in which *postremo* happens to introduce the prevailing or conclusive unit; occasionally, the host unit of *postremo* even overrules all units which precede. An important characteristic, however, which all sequences in which *postremo* is involved display, is that these preceding units are all explicitly present in the preceding context. As will turn out in the next section, this characteristic constitutes one of the crucial differences with *tandem.* A second important characteristic of *postremo* is its insensitivity to the illocutionary functions of its host unit.

3. *Tandem:* a first characterization

The description of *postremo* given in the previous section will serve as a starting-point for a contrastive comparison with *tandem,* which will result in a first characterization of this discourse particle. In 3.2 I will give an overview of the various functions of *tandem,* which will be discussed in more detail in sections 4 - 6.

3.1 Tandem and postremo: *a contrastive comparison*

On the face of it, *postremo* and *tandem* seem to be roughly comparable, at least in their 'temporal' uses. They share a semantic feature of 'ultimateness' or 'finality', and they are in some instances characterized as more or less synonymous.[11] As an illustration of the semantic overlap between *tandem* and *postremo,* compare the following two very similar utterances in which they are used. This 'minimal pair' forms a good startingpoint for a first, contrastive characterization of *tandem.*

11. See note 4.

(15)   (The *miles*, Pyrgopolynices, is telling his slave Palaestrio how difficult it was
       to convince his former mistress that she had to leave)
       PY: Quod volui ut volui impetravi, per amicitiam et gratiam,
       a Philocomasio. *(Paleastrio then expresses his surprise that it took so long; the
       miles explains that this is caused by the fact that she loves him so much)*
       PA: Quid iam? PY: Ut multa verba feci, ut lenta materies fuit!
       Verum *postremo* impetravi ut volui. (Pl. *Mil.* 1200-1204)
       'Well, Philocomasium has granted my wish just as I wished, in all friend-
       liness and good will # (...) # How is that? # How I did have to talk and talk!
       what stubborn stuff she was to deal with. However, I *finally* gained my
       point in the way I wished.'

(16)   (Lesbonicus has ordered his slave Stasimus to go to his sister in Callicles'
       house and tell her that her marriage has been arranged. Lesbonicus himself
       agrees to join the *senex* Philto elsewhere, but instead of leaving, he goes on
       giving Stasimus additional instructions:)
       LE: *(to Stasimus)* Tu istuc cura quod iussi. Ego iam hic ero.
       Dic Callicli me ut conveniat. ST: Quin tu i modo.
       LE: de dote ut videat quid opus sit facto. ST: I modo.
       LE: Nam .... ST: Quin tu i modo.
       LE: Neque enim .... ST: Abi modo.
       LE: ... ST: I modo. LE: ...
       ... ST: I modo. LE: ...
       ... ST: I modo, i modo, i modo. *(Lesbonicus leaves)*
       Tandem impetravi abiret. (Pl. *Trin.* 582-591)
       'You take care to do what I ordered. I shall soon be back here. Tell Callicles
       to meet me. # Yes, yes, only you go now. # So as to see what must be done
       about the dowry. # Only do go! # For ... # Yes, yes, only you go now! # No
       indeed ... # Just do go! # ... # Just go! # ... # Only do go! # Just go! do go!
       just go! *At last* I've got him to be gone.'

In these examples both *tandem* and *postremo* signal that the event described in their
host units is somehow 'final' and forms the last stage in a connected sequence of
events. When we take a closer look, however, there are also important differences.
Postremo serves to introduce the *miles*' success in an objective, sequential manner.
It forms the last stage in a series of connected events that are explicitly listed in the
context. Furthermore, the positive outcome of the whole process has already been
announced in the first utterance of the *miles* quoted here *(quod volui ut volui
impetravi)*, and does not require special attention in itself. *Tandem*, on the other
hand, is not primarily used to introduce the speaker's success in getting the

addressee off-stage as the last stage of an objectively described sequence of events; in fact, the stages that precede the addressee's going off-stage, are not reported by the speaker, but take place before his (and the spectator's) eyes. Instead, *tandem* serves to express the speaker's evaluation of his success as the ultimate realization of a state of affairs that he had expected to be realized earlier. The expectations on which this evaluation is based remain implicit; they ensue from the addressee's (i.e. Lesbonicus') intention to leave, which is implied in his statement that he will be back soon (*ego iam hic ero*, l. 582). These expectations are, however, clearly frustrated by the subsequent behaviour of the Lesbonicus.

That the functions of *tandem* and *postremo* are quite different can also be deduced from the fact that the two particles can be combined in one and the same utterance:

(17)   (Q. Minucius' camp is attacked at night by the *Ligures*)
Prima luce duabus simul portis eruptionem fecit. Nec primo impetu, *quod speraverat*, Ligures pulsi sunt; duas amplius horas dubium certamen sustinuere; *postremo*, cum alia atque alia agmina erumperent, et integri fessis succederent ad pugnam, *tandem* Ligures, inter cetera etiam vigiliis confecti, terga dederunt. (Liv. 36.38.3-4)
'At daybreak he made a sally through two gates at once. But the first attack did not, *as he had hoped*, drive away the Ligures; for two hours longer they made the issue uncertain; *finally*, when column after column came forth and fresh men were relieving the exhausted in the battle, the Ligures, *at last*, worn out by loss of sleep, along with everything else, turned to flight.'

The function of *postremo* in this example is, again, straightforwardly connective. It is used, at the representational level, to introduce the defeat of the *Ligures* as the last stage in a description of a battle.[12] The host unit of *postremo* thus forms the last unit of a sequence of events that are all explicitly listed. *Tandem*, on the other hand, is used here to present an evaluation of this same event (viz. the defeat of the *Ligures*) in the light of prior expectations (in this case those of Q. Minucius). More in particular, *tandem* signals here that this event is evaluated as the final or ultimate realization of what had been expected to happen earlier. Although such expec-

---

12. As has been pointed out by e.g. Witte (1910: 393-396), Walsh (1961: 197-199) and Chausserie-Laprée (1969: 24-29), Livy often makes use of sequential markers to describe a whole battle scene in terms of two or three decisive stages. In this manner, a complex event consisting of a great number of partly overlapping and partly not directly sequential actions is schematically reduced to a symmetrical list of successive stages, which usually ends with the approach of victory or the flight of one of the parties in combat.

tations often remain implicit (cf. 16), they are explicitly referred to in this example *(nec primo impetu, quod speraverat, Ligures pulsi sunt).*

The first and most important difference between the two particles is, therefore, that *tandem* is not used, as *postremo* is, to indicate coherence relations between its host unit and other units that are explicitly given in the surrounding discourse. Instead, it relates its host unit to prior expectations that are, at best, hinted at in the surrounding context, but may also remain implicit. In the terminology of Kroon (1995: 63-64; 281-284) *tandem* is not a connective particle in a strict sense, but a 'situating' or 'evaluative' particle.

A second important difference between *tandem* and *postremo* pertains to their integration in their host unit. Like *postremo*, *tandem* is a discourse marker, and not a temporal adjunct (cf. section 2.1): *tandem* does not form part of the propositional content of its host unit; it cannot occur in isolation (e.g. as the answer to a question); it is never topic or focus, and it cannot be modified.[13] Nevertheless, there are a number of indications that the function of *tandem* is more closely linked up with the individual speech acts in which it is used than *postremo* is.

A first indication, which will be ilustrated in more detail in the next sections, is that the actual function which *tandem* fulfils in individual instances is more sensitive to illocutionary and semantic properties of its host unit. As we saw in section 1, its function in rhetorical questions such as (1) differs from its function in an assertion such as (2), which in turn differs from its function in other types of assertions such as (4) and (5). *Postremo*, on the other hand, is insensitive to the illocutionary function of its host unit, as we saw in section 2.3.

Secondly, *postremo* may introduce larger host units that consist of series of (various) speech acts.[14] This is an indication of the fact that its discourse function is independent from illocutionary properties of the single speech acts that make up the host unit of *postremo*. The host units of *tandem*, on the other hand, invariably consist of single speech acts, which is at least consistent with the idea that its function is somehow more closely connected with properties of the speech acts involved.

The involvement of *tandem* in the speech act to which it belongs seems, furthermore, to be indicated by its position, as is also illustrated in example (17). While *postremo* is most commonly found in first position, which can be taken as an indication of its more independent status vis-à-vis the (series of) speech acts which it introduces, the position of *tandem* is most often inside or even at the end of the clause.

---

13. However, it seems possible to emphasize *tandem*, as in example (22) in section 4.2, where *tandem* (in combination with *percipias*) seems to be contrasted with *olim*.
14. Or units that are smaller than a single speech act, cf. examples (9) and (12) above.

My preliminary conclusion, then, is that *tandem* is not a 'connective', but an 'evaluative' discourse particle. Its function is to evaluate its host units, which always correspond with single speech acts, in terms of alternative expectations. Most commonly, these expectations remain implicit and are only evoked by the use of this particle, but they may also be referred to, or hinted at, in the surrounding context. More in particular, *tandem* marks that its host unit is evaluated as being somehow 'final' or 'ultimate' as compared to the implicit alternative expectations that are evoked by the use of *tandem*.

3.2 An overview of the uses of tandem

The preliminary characterization of *tandem* given at the end of the previous section is deliberately vague in at least two respects, viz. first, whose expectations are involved, and, secondly, in which sense the host unit of *tandem* is evaluated as being 'ultimate' or 'final'. In fact, the diversity of the functions of *tandem* results precisely from the various possibilities in these two respects, especially the latter. A number of different funtions can be distinguished, which share a relatively abstract 'basic meaning' (evaluation as 'final' or 'ultimate' as compared to implicit alternative expectations) but differ in these other respects.

As regards the former question, the expectations on which the evaluation signalled by *tandem* is based are, as we will see, most commonly those which the speaker himself entertains in performing the speech act to which *tandem* belongs. As a consequence, *tandem* functions in those cases as an interactional discourse particle, which expresses a coherence relation between its host unit and the attitude, beliefs and expectations of one of the participants in the ongoing interaction (cf. section 2.2 above). An exception is formed by a number of cases in which the expectations involved belong to (a person in) the extra-linguistic world that is described in the utterance, as in (17) above. This situation of 'described' expectations is, however, only found in a restricted group of cases, namely those in which so-called 'temporal' *tandem* (see below) pertains to the past realization of an expected event in the 'represented' extra-linguistic world. I will return to these instances in section 4.

A further, and more important distinction between the various functions of *tandem* can be made on the basis of the second point of difference, viz. in which sense the host unit of *tandem* is evaluated as being 'ultimate' or 'final'. I want to emphasize in advance that the various functions that can be distinguished are not in all cases neatly separated, but display some overlap. All in all, three clusters of functions can be distinguished. First, there is a connected chain of 'temporal' functions (discussed in section 4) in which the evaluation indicated by *tandem* pertains to the actual realization of a particular event that is somehow expected.

This temporal use ranges from instances in which this event has taken place in a past extra-linguistic world to instances in which *tandem* is used to evaluate the realization of a communicative event that belongs to the ongoing interaction. Secondly, *tandem* is used to indicate the speaker's evaluation of a totally unexpected event. This 'expressive function' will be dealt with in section 5. Section 6, finally, deals with the most difficult, 'considerative' function which *tandem* fulfils in a rather heterogeneous group of cases in which it is used to evaluate the content of a speech act as the 'ultimate thing' to say after having taken all alternatives implicitly into consideration.

4. 'Temporal' *tandem*

The most straightforward and perspicuous instances of *tandem* are those in which it signals an evaluation that is somehow temporal in nature. In these instances the evaluation pertains to the final realization of a particular event that was, for whatever reason, already expected to be realized. By using *tandem* the speaker evokes alternative, usually implicit expectations concerning the moment of realization; it signals that the actual moment of realization is 'beyond' these expectations. The use of *tandem* evokes this whole complex of prior expectations, unexpected delay, and 'ultimate' realization 'after all', as is most clearly illustrated by example (17) discussed in the previous section. The translation 'at last' or 'finally' is usually adequate to convey this, together with the emotions that may ensue from it: frustration and/or disappointment at the delay, followed by relief at the final realization.[15]

---

15. In cases in which the ultimate realization (and the accompanying relief) is emphasized, *tandem* may be combined with *aliquando*, as in example (2) and in:

> A.d. V Kal. Dec. servus Cn. Planci Brundisi *tandem aliquando* mihi a te expecta-tissimas litteras reddit datas Id. Nov., quae me molestia valde levarunt; (Cic. *Fam.* 16.9.2; to Tiro)
> 'At Brundisium on 26 November a slave of C, Plancius gave me *at long last* the letter from you that I had so long been waiting for so impatiently, dispatched on the Ides of November. It greatly relieved my anxiety;'

When, on the other hand, it is the unexpected delay that has postponed the expected realization (and the ensuing frustration) that is emphasized, we may find adverbs such as *aegre* and *aegerrime* 'with (very) great difficulty' or *vix* 'hardly, with great effort', combined with *tandem*:

> *Vix tandem* legi litteras dignas Ap. Claudio, plenas humanitatis officio diligentiae; aspectus videlicet urbis tibi tuam pristinam urbanitatem reddidit. Nam quas ex itinere ante quam ex Asia egressus est ad me litteras misisti (...) legi perinvitus; (Cic. *Fam.* 3.9.1)
> 'Well, *at long last* I have read a letter worthy of Appius Claudius, full of courtesy, friendliness, and consideration! It would seem that the sight of Rome has given you back your old urbanity. For I was very sorry to read the letters you sent me *en route* before you left Asia (...);'

Under the heading of 'temporal *tandem*' a number of different functions can be distinguished, which differ as to the nature of the event evaluated and the question whose expectations are involved. As regards the nature of the event evaluated, we can distinguish a 'chain' of usages, which ranges from events in the extra-linguistic world, which are evaluated in assertions and exclamations (cf. section 4.1), via future extra-linguistic events whose realization is ordered in directive speech acts (cf. section 4.2) to discourse-internal, verbal actions that are elicited in questions (cf. section 4.3).

4.1 Factual events

Example (17) is a good example of a factual, extra-linguistic event whose actual realization is described in an assertion and evaluated by means of *tandem*. Most commonly the event involved is telic, and more often than not it is described in a past tense. In such past instances, the expectations involved need not be the expectations which the speaker entertains at the moment of speaking, but they may also belong to the extra-linguistic world that is described in the utterance involved and its surrounding context. This was e.g. the case in (17), where the expectations on which the evaluation is based are those of Minucius, and not the speaker's. More or less similar are those instances in which the expectations involved were the speaker's, but do belong to the past described world, not to the present communicative situation, as in:

(18) (Hegio describes how much people appreciated his buying a group of captives)
      HE: (...) ubi quisque vident,
      eunt obviam gratulanturque eam rem.
      Ita me miserum restitando retinendoque lassum reddiderunt:
      vix ex gratulando miser iam eminebam.
      Tandem abii ad praetorem; (Pl. *Capt.* 500-505)
      'whenever anyone sees me, up he comes and congratulates me on it! Dear, dear! I was so worn out with all their stopping and detaining me, it got to be frightfully hard work emerging from the flood of felicitations. *At last* I escaped to the praetor's.'

There seems, then, to be a difference with other instances of 'temporal' *tandem*, in which the expectations involved are those which the speaker entertains in speaking. For instance in (2) and (16), repeated here, the speaker discusses an event that has taken place immediately before speaking (cf. 16) or whose impact belongs to the present situation (as in 2).

(2)   *Tandem* aliquando (...) L. Catilinam (...) ex urbe vel eiecimus vel emisimus
      vel ipsum egredientem verbis prosecuti sumus. Abiit, excessit, evasit, erupit.
      (Cic. *Catil.* 2.1)

(16) *Tandem* impetravi abiret. (Pl. *Trin.* 591)

On the basis of this difference, one could be inclined to consider the former type,
in which the expectations belong to the 'described' world, as instances in which
tandem fulfils a 'representational' function (cf. section 2.2), as opposed to all other
cases where *tandem* is an interactional discourse particle, because it connects its
host unit with expectations that form part of the communicative situation.
However, the borderline between such 'representational' temporal uses and
'interactional' temporal uses would not be very clear. Moreover, and more
importantly, even those cases in which *tandem* is used to evoke an evaluation that
is based on such 'external' expectations, *tandem* does seem to lend a 'subjective'
tone to the evaluation: in all instances, the 'external expectations' seem to be shared
by the speaker, either because they are his own past expectations or because they
belonged to those with whom the speaker identifies himself (e.g. a Roman
commander such as Minucius, never a hostile commander!). Therefore, I propose
to regard *tandem* in all its uses as an interactional discourse particle, which
connects its host unit with the expectations which the speaker entertains at the
moment of speaking or with expectations that are recalled and/or identified with
by the speaker.
     It is, in this connection, not irrelevant that the use of *tandem* in descriptions
of a past situation which involves 'external expectations' often creates an effect of
suspense. Because the use of *tandem* evokes and revives the expectations involved,
the whole situation is described in a more lively way. This is clearly illustrated by
the following example, where the use of *tandem* connects the arrival of the *nuntius*
with an only very indeterminate sense of expectation that is implied in the use of
the preceding imperfects and in the *silentium longum*, viz. the expectation that
something is going to happen. *Tandem*'s function is to evoke this sense of expectation in retrospect in a much livelier way than a straightforward connective
particle such as *tum* or *postremo* would have done.[16]

(19) Sedebant iudices, decemviri venerant, observabantur advocati; silentium
      longum, *tandem* a praetore nuntius. (Plin. *Ep.* 5.9.2)

---

16. A similar example is found in Pl. *Capt.* 508-510. Cf. also Rosén's observation on the use of the
tenses in (19). The description of the situation in court is presented by means of imperfects, which
are followed by two verbless sentences, of which "the first belongs to the imperfect-context exposition, the second — by virtue of the connective *tandem* — to the narrative" (Rosén 1980: 42).

'The jurors had taken their seats, the presiding magistrates were arrived, the opposing counsel had taken their places; a long silence followed; *at last* a messenger from the praetor arrived.'

Instances in which the interactional nature of *tandem* can be most clearly observed are exclamations. Because they constitute, by definition, reactions to an event that takes place before the speaker's eyes, or of which the speaker has just been informed, the evaluation signalled by 'temporal' *tandem* in exclamations is necessarily always based on the expectations which the speaker himself entertains at the moment of speaking. The attention is usually focussed on the unexpected delay, and as a consequence the use of *tandem* usually reinforces negative emotions (anger or frustration) that are already present in the exclamation. Examples are the exclamation in (20) and the 'reproaching question' (*i.e.* a rhetorical question with a reproaching tenor) under (21). (20) forms part of an emotional passage which as a whole clearly betrays the speaker's frustration at the behaviour of the *lena* (cf. also the invective *inlecebram*). In (21) *tandem* directly pertains to the unexpected lateness of the addressee's arrival, and thus reinforces the reproaching tone of this question.[17]

(20) (Argyrippus is angrily shouting at the house of the *lena* Cleareta, who has just thrown him out of her house, because he is out of money)
      At scelesta viden ut ne id quidem me dignum esse existumat
      quem adeat, quem conloquatur quoique irato supplicet?
      Atque eccam inlecebram exit *tandem*; (Pl. *As.* 149-151)
      'But d'ye see how the wretch doesn't even think it worth while to come to me, talk with me, go on her knees to me, when I'm in a rage? *(Cleareta's door opens)* But look, there she is coming out *at last*, the decoy;'

(21) TO: Redis tu *tandem*? DO: Redeo. (Pl. *Per.* 733)
      'Back *finally*, are you? # Back I am.'

---

17. The comment on this utterance by Woytek (1982, ad loc.) nicely emphasizes the subjective nature of the speaker's evaluation signalled by *tandem*: "*tandem* nach einer nur 7 Verse währenden Abwesenheit der angeredeten Person erlaubt weder (...) die Vermutung, Plautus habe das Original (..) verkürzt, noch erklärt (...) dichterische Freiheit alles. Vielmehr ist die Diskrepanz zwischen der objektiv kurzen Abwesenheit der Dordalus (...) und deren Einschätzung durch Toxilus sogar ein besonders feiner Zug, (...)". Comparable instances are e.g. Ter. *An.* 586, and Apul. *Met.* 6.8; 6.9.

4.2 Non-factual events

In the types of speech acts that were discussed above (assertions and expressive speech acts) the evaluation signalled by 'temporal' *tandem* concerns the realization of an event that has actually taken place in the extra-linguistic world. However, the 'temporal evaluation' may also pertain to the realization of an event that has not yet taken place, but is ordered or requested in a directive speech act, and thus forms the 'communicative goal' of the speaker in performing his speech act. There is a gradual transition from the temporal evaluation of 'factual events' in assertive and expressive speech acts, via a related use in final and consecutive clauses (cf. 22), to directives (cf. 23):

(22) Et de editione quidem interim, ut voles; recita saltem, quo magis libeat emittere, utque *tandem* percipias gaudium, quod ego olim pro te non temere praesumo. (Plin. *Ep.* 2.10.6)
'However, as to publishing them, have your own way for the present. But let me at least prevail with you to recite them, that you may be more disposed to send them abroad; and may receive *at last* that satisfaction, which I, upon very just grounds, have been expecting for you for a long time.'

(23) (Psyche addresses her mourning sisters, who think that she is dead)
Et "Quid" inquit "vos miseris lamentationibus nequiquam effligitis? Quam lugetis, adsum. Lugubres voces desinite et diutius lacrimis madentes genas siccate *tandem*, quippe cum iam possitis quam plangebatis amplecti." (Apul. *Met.* 5.7)
'"Why needlessly destroy yourselves" she cried "with pitiful lamentation? I, whom you are mourning, am here. Stop those mournful sounds and *at last* dry your cheeck soaked so long in tears, for you can now embrace the girl for whom you were grieving."'

It is important to note that, in (23), the expectations of the speaker on which her temporal evaluation is based here do not stem from the performance of the directive itself, but are implied to have been already on her mind at the moment of performing the directive. It is precisely this (implied) feeling that the state of affairs involved 'should already have been realized' (cf. also the comparative *diutius*) which urges the speaker to use *tandem*. Not surprisingly, *tandem* is often found in directives which repeat an earlier directive that was not complied with.[18]

---

18. Cf. e.g. Pl. *Capt.* 964; Ter *An.* 895. Or in directives that form a reaction to a habitual behaviour, to which the speaker will have reacted more often in the past, as e.g. in Ter. *Ad.* 794.

4.3 Communicative events

While the communicative goal of a directive is the realization of an extra-linguistic event which is specified in the content of the directive, the speaker's communicative goal in asking a question[19] is the realization of a discourse-internal, 'communicative event': The aim of asking a question is to make the addressee give an answer in which he supplies the information asked for in the question. When a speaker uses *tandem* in a question, he evaluates the 'realization' of the answer in terms of his prior, implicit expectations that he would have received the information asked for already earlier. There is, therefore, an important difference with the function of *tandem* in directives: in questions, *tandem* does not pertain to the 'content' of the question, but only to the communicative act of answering the question.

As is illustrated in (24), questions containing *tandem* often follow on a previous 'informative act' by the addressee (here: *nil equidem nisi quod illum audivi dicere* 'it's only what I heard him say'): they concern the specification of additional information, which the speaker had expected to be given right away (here the information *what* the *senex* was saying), or at least earlier. This explains the impatient tone which *tandem* usually lends to such questions.[20]

(24) DA: (...)
Nescioquis senex modo venit, ellum, confidens catus:
quom faciem videas, videtur esse quantivis preti:
tristi' severitas inest in voltu atque in verbis fides.
SI: Quidnam adportas? DA: Nil equidem nisi quod illum audivi dicere.
SI: *Quid ait tandem?* DA: Glycerium se scire civem esse Atticam. SI: Hem.
(Ter. *An.* 855-859)
'Some old gentleman came just now, what a man! all brass and cunning. To look at him you'd think him worth his weight in gold, his face all sombre truthfulness and his voice enough to make you believe him. # What's your story now? # I've no story, sir, it's only what I heard him say # And *tell me* what does he say? # That he knows that Glycerium is a citizen of Athens # Oh, I see.'

There are two instances in my corpus of questions containing *quid tandem* in which the speaker does not ask for additional details in connection with previously

---

19. I mean a 'real question', *i.e.* not just any interrogative sentence, but only those interrogatives whose illocutionary force is aimed at obtaining information (most commonly from the addressee), cf. Risselada (1993: 37-43). Example (21) above, for instance, is not a real question, but an expressive (reproaching) speech act.
20. Similar example are Pl. *Mos.* 1000; 1108; and Ter. *Ph.* 798.

given information, but opens an interactional exchange on a particular discourse topic right away with an impatient *quid tandem* question. One of them is taken from Cicero's *De oratore* 2.12-13, where the narration proper is continued after the prologue.[21] On the morning of the second day, Catulus and his brother suddenly arrive; their arrival causes astonishment and curiosity:

(25)   Qui cum inter se, ut ipsorum usus ferebat, amicissime consalutassent: '*quid vos tandem?*' Crassus 'num quidnam' inquit 'novi?' 'Nihil sane,' inquit Catulus '(...)' (Cic. *de Orat.* 2.12-13)
'After exchanging very cordial greetings with one another, as their practice was, Crassus inquired, "Out with it: what brings you here? Have you any news?" "None whatever", replied Catulus, "(...)"'

Here the *tandem* question does not continue an earlier conversation, but it is prompted by the unexpected arrival which, in view of the political tension in Rome, is taken as an indication that there may be new developments. In this sense, the question does ask for 'additional' (or 'more specific') information and *tandem* emphasizes Crassus' impatience in 'finally' receiving this information, after the preliminary greetings have been exchanged.[22]

Besides this 'chain' of temporal uses, in which the scope of the evaluation signalled by *tandem* ranges from actually realized extra-linguistic events to intended communicative actions, *tandem* is also used in two, quite different 'non-temporal' senses, to which I will turn now.

---

21. The other example is Ter. *Ad.* 276, where a conversation opened by *quid ait tandem nobis Sannio?* continues an earlier conversation.
22. As was pointed out to me (Jan de Jong, p.c.) this particular use of *tandem* could also be interpreted as an instance of the 'expressive' use to be discussed in the next section. Interestingly, however, we find a very similar onset of a conversation in the *Brutus*, which takes place under comparable circumstances of political tension.
    Quos postquam salutavi: 'Quid vos' inquam, 'Brute et Attice? numquid *tandem* novi?' 'Nihil sane' inquit Brutus '(...)'. (Cic. *Brut.* 10)
    'I greeted them and began abruptly: "How now, Brutus, and you, Atticus. Any news yet *tandem*?" "No, nothing", replied Brutus, "(...)".'
In this instance, *tandem* is not found in the opening question *quid vos* (which seems to constitute a more general question about the addressee's condition than is the case in the *De oratore* instance quoted above), but in the subsequent, more specific question *numquid tandem novi?* In both cases, however, *tandem* serves to underline the speaker's urgency to be informed.

5. 'Expressive' *tandem*

In the first of the two 'non-temporal' uses, *tandem* signals the speaker's evaluation of an unexpected event in the extra-linguistic world. Most commonly this event is a non-telic event that takes place before the speaker's eyes or a (telic or non-telic) past event that has just been brought to his attention. Because the event involved was not expected, the evaluation cannot pertain to its (long-awaited) moment of realization. Instead, *tandem* is used to evaluate the event itself as compared to the implicit expectations of the speaker as to what could have happened. The event is evaluated as 'beyond' his expectations.

The difference with the uses discussed earlier can be illustrated by comparing the following two instances, the former 'temporal', the latter non-temporal, or 'expressive' as I label this particular use:

(21)   TO: Redis tu *tandem*? DO: Redeo. (Pl. *Per.* 733)
       'Back *finally*, are you? # Back I am.'

(26)   (speaker and addressee are discussing the ownership of a trunk, which the
       addressee has caught fishing, and now claims to be his)
                     TR: Quid ais, impudens?
       Ausu's etiam comparare vidulum cum piscibus?
       Eadem *tandem* res videtur? (Pl. *Rud.* 981-983)
       'How's that, you cheeky rascal? So you've got the cheek to compare trunks
       with fish, eh? Do they seem the same to you? *Really?*'

In the former, the returning of the addressee *(tu)* had been expected by the speaker, and *tandem* signals the speaker's evaluation of *when* this situation is actually realized as compared to his implicit expectations with respect to the moment of realization. In the latter, on the other hand, the use of *tandem* signals the speaker's evaluation of the event in itself (*i.e.* the addressee's entertaining a particular opinion), as compared to *what* the speaker had expected to happen. By using *tandem* the speaker evokes an implicit comparison with possible alternative situations, compared to which the event involved is evaluated as the most unlikely and the least expected situation, that is, as the 'last thing' the speaker had expected to happen (for whatever reason) or even as something that is 'beyond expectation'.

In a number of instances of this 'expressive' function, we find *tandem* combined with for instance *nimis* (cf. 5 in section 1) which similarly, and independently, signals that the event evaluated occupies an extreme position on a scale of expectedness, or is even beyond this scale. However, as we see in (26), *tandem* can also have this function when it is not combined with a scalar expression.

The speaker's judgement of the event evaluated is most commonly negative:[23]

(27) Itane *tandem* uxorem duxit Antipho iniussu meo?
Nec meum imperium — ac mitto imperium —, non simultatem meam revereri saltem! non pudere! o facinus audax, o Geta. (Ter. *Ph.* 231-234)
'*What? Do you really mean* to tell me that Antipho has married a wife without my leave? What, no regard for my authority — I won't mention authority — for my indignation even? No shame either? What atrocious assurance!'

It may, however, also be positive or merely incredulous as in (28). In this instance *tandem* signals, as it does in (26), that the event evaluated is 'beyond his expectations', but *tandem* does not evoke the usual negative expectations:[24]

(28) *(the parasite Artotrogus is flattering the Miles, and describes how women talk about him; the Miles reacts surprised)*
MI: Quid eae dixerunt tibi?
AR: Rogitabant: "hicine Achilles est?" inquit mihi.
"Immo eius frater" inquam "est". Ibi illarum altera
"ergo mecastor pulcher est" inquit mihi
"et liberalis. Vide caesaries quam decet.
Ne illae sunt fortunatae quae cum isto cubant."
MI: Itane aibant *tandem*? (Pl. *Mil.* 60-66)
'What did they say to you? # They kept asking about you, sir: "Is he Achilles?" says one of them. "No, his brother" says I. "Goodness gracious! that's why he is such a fine, handsome gentleman," says the other one. "Just see what lovely hair he has. My! but the girls that cuddle him are lucky!". # Did they *really* say that, eh?'

If my analysis of (28) is correct (but see note 24), we could conclude that *tandem* itself is neutral with respect to the emotions (positive or negative) that are involved

---

23. Other instances of *itane tandem* are: Ter. *An.* 492. *Ph.* 411; 526; *Hau.* 955 ; Pl. *Trin.* 642.
24. Unless, of course, one interprets the reaction of the *miles* as expressing (feigned!) irritation at the admiration of the women. In that case (28) would simply be similar to (26). On the basis of the parasite's reaction in 66-67, however, I am inclined to interpret (28) in terms of sincere incredulity, and not yet in terms of the feigned irritation that accompanies line 68.
    Instances such as these have led Langen (1880: 88-91, *ad* Pl. *As.* 176) to take as one of the two 'meanings' of *tandem* '(denn) wirklich' ("in Fragen und Behauptungen, die eine gewisse Erregtheit, Unwillen, Verwunderung etc. bekunden"). Petersmann (1973, *ad* Pl. *St.* 765) follows Langen in this respect and explicitly refers to this instance.

,in the evaluation. It simply signals that the event evaluated is beyond whatever range of implicit expectations is evoked.

Another turn, in which *tandem* is frequently found with this expressive function is *ain tandem?*. This expression is used in incredulous reactions to the words of the addressee. An example is (29). Artemona, the wife of Demipho is overhearing a conversation between her husband and the *meretrix* Philaenium, who is kissing him. In an aside she gives an incredulous (*tandem*: 'this is the limit!') and angry (*edepol, ne tu istuc ...*) reaction to her husband's insult:

(29)   DE: Edepol animam suaviorem aliquanto quam uxoris meae.
       PH: Dic amabo, an fetet anima uxoris tuae? DE: Nauteam
       bibere malim, si necessum sit, quam illam oscularier.
       AR: [aside] *Ain tandem?* Edepol ne tu istuc cum malo magno tuo
       dixisti in me. Sine, revenias modo domum, faxo ut scias
       quid pericli sit dotatae uxori vitium dicere. (Pl. *As.* 893-898)
       'My word, that's sweeter breath than my wife's! # Do tell me, there's a dear,
       your wife's breath isn't bad, is it? # I'd rather drink bilge water, if it came
       to that, than kiss her. # So, you would, would you? *Incredible!* Good gra-
       cious sir, that fling at me will cost you dear. Very well! you just come back
       home, sir! I'll show you the danger of vilifying a wife with money.'

Although it might seem quite paradoxical that *tandem* can be used to signal both 'final realization of an expectation after an unexpected delay' (temporal *tandem*) and 'the ultimate unexpected thing' (expressive *tandem*), these two uses share the semantic basic component of 'ultimateness' (both refer to what is ultimately taking place) as well as the evoking of alternative implicit expectations, which are, albeit in different ways, frustrated.

6. 'Considerative' *tandem*

The other non-temporal use of *tandem* is quite different; in fact, it is the most difficult one to account for. In this type of use *tandem* does not pertain to (the realization of) an extra-linguistic event or a communicative action. Instead, by using *tandem* the speaker evaluates a speech act (usually his own) in terms of the implicit considerations that have led him to perform it. More in particular the use of *tandem* signals that, when all relevant aspects are considered, the speech act involved is 'the ultimate' thing' the speaker has to say here. This may be a particular opinion, a proposal, or an argument for a particular argumentative claim. For want of a better term, I call this the 'considerative' function of *tandem*.

A first illustration of this function was given in (4), where *tandem* is combined rather loosely, first with an assertion and then with a rhetorical question:[25]

(4)   *sed tandem*, opinor, aequiust eram mihi esse supplicem   290
      atque oratores mittere ad me donaque ex auro et quadrigas
      qui vehar, nam pedibus ire non queo. (...)
      sed tandem quom recogito, qui potuit scire haec scire me?   301
      non enim possum quin revortar, quin loquar, quin edissertem
      eramque ex maerore eximam (...) (Pl. *St.* 290-303)

In this example, the speaker's evaluation of his own speech acts as stating the 'ultimate thing to do after considering all implicit alternatives' happens to be hinted at also by other elements: in the first line the comparative *aequiust* points to an (implicit) process of considering and comparing alternatives, from which the content conveyed forms the result, while in line 301 *quom recogito* also refers to the process of (re)considering on which the rhetorical question introduced is based.

It is insightful to compare the use of *tandem* in instances such as (4) with the use of *postremo* in seemingly comparable instances such as (12). In both cases the host unit of the particle involved is somehow the ultimate 'point' made by the speaker. However, while the function of *postremo* in (12) amounts to indicating that its host unit forms the speaker's 'final word' (*i.e.* the last of a series of explicit arguments) on the subject matter, the function of *tandem* in (4) is to indicate that its host unit forms the speaker's 'final consideration' (*i.e.* the ultimate thing to say after implicitly having considered all relevant aspects).

(12)   PH: Ohe,
      "actum" aiunt "ne agas". DE: Non agam? Immo haud desinam
      donec perfecero hoc. PH: Ineptis. DE: Sine modo.
      PH: *Postremo* tecum nil rei nobis, Demipho, est:
      tuos est damnatus gnatus, non tu; nam tua
      praeterierat iam ducendi aetas. (Ter. *Ph.* 418-423)

This use of *tandem* is mainly (but not exclusively) found in rhetorical questions, where *tandem* is notoriously difficult to account for, and is usually taken to contribute no more than an emotional overtone of urgency or impatience (cf.

---

25. As was observed in section 3.1, *tandem* usually is more integrated in the speech acts in which it is used. Here, it forms part of a relatively independent metacommunicative comment. Its function is, however, similar to its function in the other examples discussed in this section.

section 1). Although this emotional overtone is unmistakably present in many rhetorical questions containing *tandem* (but note that rhetorical questions more in general tend to have an emotional overtone), I am inclined to consider it an effect of the use of *tandem* in a particular context and situation, rather than an essential part of its function. In my opinion, the function of *tandem* in these cases is, in line with its basic meaning of 'ultimateness', to indicate that the content of the speech act involved forms the ultimate outcome of an implicit process of considering all relevant aspects and of comparing the host unit of *tandem* with all possible implicit alternatives.

As an introduction to some examples of rhetorical questions, I will first deal with an instance of *tandem* in an indirect, more or less 'real' question. The utterance as a whole forms the beginning of a new paragraph and it introduces the discourse topic of this paragraph, viz. 'which evidence can be inferred from the *locus ad insidias*':

(3) Videamus nunc id, quod caput est, locus ad insidias ille ipse, ubi congressi sunt, utri *tandem* fuerit aptior. (Cic. *Mil.* 53)

In view of the question nature of the clause containing *tandem*, the particle evokes here not so much the speaker's considerations in asking this question, but the considerations on the basis of which ('all things considered, after all') the ultimate answer to this question should be given. In fact, it could be maintained that it is the very use of *tandem* which lends a certain 'rhetorical' overtone to this question; by evoking a careful process of taking into consideration all relevant aspects, the speaker implicitly conveys that these considerations do lead to the conclusion that the location was indeed more suitable for the one (*scil.* Clodius) than for the other (*scil.* Milo). Now compare a fully rhetorical question such as:

(30) Faveo aratori, cupio octupli damnari Apronium. Quid *tandem* postulat arator? Nihil nisi ex edicto iudicium in octuplum. (Cic. *Ver.* 3,28)
      'We are for the farmer, and hope that Apronius will be sentenced to make eightfold restitution. What is the farmer's petition, *after all*? Simply the right to sue for eightfold restitution as the edict directs.'

As in (3), *tandem*, strictly speaking, evokes the process of 'considerations' that should underly the answer to the question posed. In view, however, of the unambiguous rhetorical nature of the question, and of the fact that the answer (in this case actually spelled out in the next utterance: 'nothing unreasonable or against the law') is already implied in the rhetorical question itself, *tandem* evokes here the speaker's own process of taking all relevant considerations into account and considering the content conveyed as the ultimate one, as compared to all implicit alternatives.

In (30) the host unit of *tandem* fulfils the function of an argument by means of which the speaker supports his claim that he is on the side of the farmer and against Apronius, Verres' partner in squeezing money from the Sicilian farmers *(faveo aratori, cupio octupli damnari Apronium)*. In view of the function of *tandem*, which is to mark the content of the rhetorical question as the ultimate outcome of an implicit process of considering all relevant facts and of comparing it with all possible alternative contents, it also marks its host unit as the ultimate argument for this claim.[26] This argumentative value is, however, only a side-effect of the primarily considerative function of *tandem* in combination with the discourse constellation in which it is used, as can be seen in instances like (3) and (30) above, where *tandem* is used in other discourse constellations and does not have this argumentative value.[27]

Another example of the considerative function of *tandem* in a slightly different discourse constellation is (31). It exemplifies the use of *tandem* in an *a fortiori* reasoning, where it evokes, as a consequence of its considerative function, all the implicit alternatives that are 'surpassed' by the 'ultimate' claim made here:

(31) Ac si nos, id quod maxime debet, nostra patria delectat, cuius rei tanta est vis
      ac tanta natura, ut Ithacam illam in asperrimis saxulis tamquam nidulum
      adfixam sapientissimus vir immortalitati anteponeret, quo amore *tandem*
      inflammati esse debemus in eius modi patriam, quae una in omnibus terris
      domus est virtutis, imperi, dignitatis? (Cic. *de Orat.* 1.196)
      'And if our own native land is our joy, as to the uttermost it ought to be,
      — a sentiment of such strength and quality that a hero of consummate
      prudence gave preference over immortality to "that Ithaca of his, lodged like
      a tiny nest upon the roughest of small crags" — with love how ardent
      tandem must we surely be fired for a country such as ours, standing alone

---

26. Other examples are Pl. *Truc.* 238; *Men.* 712; en Lucr. 1.378.

    Cf. French *en fin de compte* or its Dutch literal equivalent *per slot van rekening*, which are, unlike *tandem*, both exclusively used in subordinate discourse acts that support a preceding claim. Marking their host unit as the 'ultimate argument for a claim' is, therefore, their primary function, and not a side-effect that derives from a particular discourse constellation, as is the case for *tandem*.

27. Occasionally, we find this 'argumentative side-effect' also in other types of speech acts than rhetorical questions. An example is Pl. *As.* 176, where *tandem* fulfils the same 'considerative' function of evaluating the speech act as the speaker's 'ultimate' step, after implicitly considering alternative arguments for the fact that the addressee (a *lena*) should be careful with the speaker.

    Ussing (1875: 367-368), who follows Donatus' suggestion *ad* Ter. *Eun.* 1055, proposes to interpret *tandem* here as equivalent to *saltem* 'at least', but that is an unnecessary step: the 'considerative' function of *tandem* in this example fits in very well with the other examples given here.

among all lands as the home of the excellence, imperial power and good report!'

Along these lines, the use of *tandem* can be explained in a large number of rhetorical questions, without having to accept that *tandem* does no more than adding impatient emphasis to the utterance involved. To my mind, the impatient emotional tone which is, indeed, often found in rhetorical questions containing *tandem* is always a side-effect that ensues from the actual function (temporal, expressive or considerative) of *tandem* in combination with properties of the verbal and non-verbal context, and does not constitute the 'meaning' of *tandem*. This brings us back to the first example in section 1.

7. *Quo usque tandem ...?*

I will conclude this paper by reconsidering the function of *tandem* in the opening line of Cicero's first Catilinarian:

(1)   Quo usque *tandem* abutere, Catilina, patientia nostra?

If we want to determine the function of *tandem*, we will first have to decide what type of speech act is performed by means of this rhetorical question , and what is Cicero's communicative goal in performing this speech act.

If the utterance is primarily meant as an expressive speech act, by means of which Cicero wants to express his mere disapproval of the abject behaviour of Catilina, this would probably be an instance of what I have labelled 'expressive' *tandem* (cf. section 5): it expresses Cicero's incredulity and his evaluation that this behaviour is worse than he could have imagined.

If, on the other hand, the speech act serves a further communicative goal, and is intended as an indirect directive to stop this behaviour, the use of *tandem* could also be described as 'temporal' (cf. section 4): Cicero expresses his impatience by evaluating the content of his directive as something that should have been realized already much earlier. In both the temporal and the expressive analysis, the rhetorical questions that follow the opening line can be interpreted as arguments for the (either directive or merely expressive) speech act performed.

However, the utterance could perhaps also be analyzed as an instance of the 'considerative' use of *tandem* discussed in the previous section: 'how long will you, *all things considered*, continue to abuse our patience?'. Under this analysis, the opening line can be taken either as an ultimate argument for the implicit claim:

'you position is becoming untenable', or as an independent claim 'you will not be able to abuse our patience much longer'.

How can we choose between these three possibilities? We probably cannot choose — and we shouldn't. By using *tandem* in his opening line Cicero evokes all connotations than are connected with these three functions: incredulity and rejection (ensuing from the 'expressive analysis'); frustration and impatience (ensuing from the 'temporal analysis'); and perhaps also the selfevident authority that ensues from the 'considerative analysis'. As such, the 'meaning' of *tandem* in this particular instance consists, indeed, of the emotions that are conveyed. But this is not the inherent meaning of *tandem* in itself: it is a combined effect of the very emotional non-verbal context of this speech and the use of *tandem* in an opening line, while in all of its functions it presupposes expectations and hence a preceding context. Therefore, the most important function of *tandem* in this opening line is to suggest that it is not an opening line at all, but part of an ongoing discourse, in which Cicero reacts to the behaviour of Catilina.

The opening line of the first Catilinarian is not only for us one of the most famous quotations from Latin, but it was so already in Antiquity. It is, for instance, no coincidence[28] that we find the phrase *quo usque tandem* in Sallust's portrait of Catiline, in a speech which the latter addresses to his fellow conjurers:

(32)   (...) Itaque omnis gratia, potentia, honos, divitiae apud illos sunt aut ubi illi volunt; nobis reliquere pericula, repulsas, iudicia, egestatem. *Quae quousque tandem patiemini, o fortissumi viri?* Nonne emori per virtutem praestat quam vitam miseram atque inhonestam, ubi alienae superbiae ludibrio fueris, per dedecus amittere? (...) (Sal. *Cat.* 20.8-9)
       'Because of this, all influence, power, rank, and wealth are in their hands, or wherever they wish them to be; to us they have left danger, defeat, prosecutions, and poverty. *How long, in heaven's name, will you endure this, brave hearts?* Is it not better to die valiantly, than ignominiously to lose our wretched and dishonoured lives after being the sport of other's insolence?'

Both the immediately following lines and the rest of the speech make clear what the function of *tandem* is here. The utterance has, on its own, clearly a directive tenor, and by means of 'temporal *tandem*' the speaker conveys his impatience that his addressees have not yet stopped enduring the situation. If, in spite of this unambiguousness, the use of *tandem* in this speech brings along also the other

---

28. Although opinions differ as to the question whether the echo is a parody (as is argued by Renehan 1976: 99-100) or an indirect compliment (cf. Innes 1977: 486).

emotions that were conveyed in (1), this is a result of the echo of Cicero's opening line, but not of the 'meaning' of *tandem*.

Bibliography

Chausserie-Laprée, J.-P.
  1969 *L'expression narrative chez les historiens latins*. Paris: De Boccard
Gutierrez Galinda, M.A.
  1989 *Denique, demum, tandem y postremo*. Estudio funcioestructural (con especial referencia a la obra lucreciana). *Emerita* 57, 263-275
Halm, K. & W. Sternkopf
  1916 *Ciceros Catilinarische Reden, erklärt van Karl Halm, besorgt von Wilh. Sternkopf*. Berlin: Weidemann
Hand, F.
  1829-1845 *Tursellinus seu de particulis Latinis commentarii* (4 vols). Leipzig: Weidemann (repr. 1969 Amsterdam: Hakkert)
Haury, A.
  1969 *Orationes in Catilinam. Édition, introduction et commentaires de Auguste Haury*. Paris: Presses Universitaires de France
Hilton, J.
  1989 Temporal connectors in the narrative discourse of Cicero. *Cahiers de l'Institut de Linguistique de Louvain* 15, 173-184
Innes, D.C.
  1977 Quo usque tandem patiemini? *Classical Quarterly* 27, 468.
Krebs, J.P. & J.H. Schmalz
  1907 *Antibarbarus der lateinischen Sprache* (2 vols). Basel (repr. 1962 Darmstadt: Wissenschaftliche Buchgesellschaft)
Kroon, C.H.M.
  1995 *Discourse Particles in Latin. A Study of* nam, enim, autem, vero *and* at. Amsterdam: Gieben
Kühner, R. & C. Stegmann
  1912-1914 *Ausführliche Grammatik der lateinischen Sprache. II Satzlehre* (2 vols). Hannover: Hahnsche Buchhandlung
Langen, P.
  1880 *Beiträge zur Kritik und Erklärung des Plautus*. Leipzig: Teubner (Repr. 1973 Hildesheim: Olms)
Nøjgaard, M.
  1992 *Les adverbes français. Essai de description fonctionelle*. Tome I. Copenhagen: Royal Danish Academy of Science and Letters.
Petersmann, H.
  1973 *T. Maccius Plautus, Stichus. Einleitung, Text, Kommentar*. Heidelberg: Winter

Renehan, R.
   1976   A traditional pattern of imitation in Sallust and his sources. *Classical Philology*
          71, 97-105
Richter, F., A. Eberhard & H. Nohl
   1912   *Ciceros Catilinarische Reden für den Schul- und Privatgebrauch erklärt von Fr.
          Richter und Alfr. Eberhard (In siebenter Auflage bearbeitet von Hermann Nohl).*
          Liepzig/Berlin: Teubner
Risselada, R.
   1993   *Imperatives and other directive Expression in Latin. A Study in the Pragmatics
          of a dead Language.* Amsterdam: Gieben
   1996   And now for something completely different? Temporal discourse markers:
          Latin *nunc* and English *now*. In: R. Risselada *et al.* (eds) *On Latin. Linguistic
          and literary Studies in Honour of Harm Pinkster.* Amsterdam: Gieben, p.105-
          125
Rosén, H.
   1980   "Exposition und Mitteilung". The Imperfect as a thematic tense-form in the
          letters of Pliny', in: Rosén, Hannah & Haiim B. Rosén *On Moods and Tenses
          of the Latin Verb. Two essays.* München: Fink, 27-48
Ussing, J.L.
   1875   *T. Maccius Plautus Comoediae. Recensuit et enarravit Iohannes Ludovicus
          Ussing.* Vol. I. Copenhagen: Hegel
Walsh, P.G.
   1961   *Livy. His historical Aims and Methods.* Cambridge, Cambridge University Press
Witte, K.
   1910   Über die Form der Darstellung in Livius' Geschichtswerk. *Rheinisches Museum*
          65, 359-419
Woytek, E.
   1982   *T. Maccius Plautus: Persa.* Vienna: Akademie Verlag

INDEX LOCORUM